I WILL GIVE YOU SHEPHERDS

PASTORES DABO VOBIS

POST-SYNODAL
APOSTOLIC EXHORTATION
MARCH 25, 1992

Addressed by the Supreme Pontiff John Paul II to the Bishops, Clergy and Faithful on the Formation of Priests in the Circumstances of the Present Day

CONTENTS

CHAPTER IV

COME AND SEE

PRIESTLY VOCATION
IN THE CHURCH'S PASTORAL WORK

CHAPTER V

HE APPOINTED TWELVE TO BE WITH HIM

THE FORMATION OF CANDIDATES
FOR THE PRIESTHOOD

CHAPTER VI

I REMIND YOU TO REKINDLE THE GIFT OF GOD THAT IS WITHIN YOU

THE ONGOING FORMATION OF PRIESTS

INTRODUCTION

1. " I WILL GIVE YOU shepherds after my own heart" (*Jer* 3:15).

In these words from the prophet Jeremiah, God promises his people that he will never leave them without shepherds to gather them together and guide them: "I will set shepherds over them [my sheep] who will care for them, and they shall fear no more, nor be dismayed" (*Jer* 23:4).

The Church, the People of God, constantly experiences the reality of this prophetic message and continues joyfully to thank God for it. She knows that Jesus Christ himself is the living, supreme and definitive fulfilment of God's promise: "I am the good shepherd" (*Jn* 10:11). He, "the great shepherd of the sheep" (*Heb* 13:20), entrusted to the Apostles and their successors the ministry of shepherding God's flock (cf. *Jn* 21:15ff.; *1 Pt* 5:2).

Without priests the Church would not be able to live that fundamental obedience which is at the very heart of her existence and her mission in history, an obedience in response to the command of Christ: "Go therefore and make disciples of all nations" (*Mt* 28:19) and "Do this in remembrance of me" (*Lk* 22:19; cf. *1 Cor* 11:24), i.e., an obedience to the command to announce the Gospel and to renew daily the sacrifice of the

3

giving of his body and the shedding of his blood for the life of the world.

By faith we know that the Lord's promise cannot fail. This very promise is the reason and force underlying the Church's rejoicing at the growth and increase of priestly vocations now taking place in some parts of the world. It is also the foundation and impulse for a renewed act of faith and fervent hope in the face of the grave shortage of priests which is being felt in other parts of the world. Everyone is called upon to share complete trust in the unbroken fulfilment of God's promise, which the Synod Fathers expressed in clear and forceful terms: "The Synod with complete trust in the promise of Christ who has said: 'Lo, I am with you always, to the close of the age' (*Mt* 28:20) and aware of the constant activity of the Holy Spirit in the Church, firmly believes that there will never be a complete lack of sacred ministers in the Church ... Even though in a number of regions there is a scarcity of clergy, the action of the Father, who raises up vocations, will nonetheless always be at work in the Church".[1]

At the conclusion of the Synod, I said that in the face of a crisis of priestly vocations "the first answer which the Church gives lies in a total act of faith in the Holy Spirit. We are deeply convinced that this trusting abandonment will not disappoint if we remain faithful to the graces we have received".[2]

[1] *Propositio* 2.
[2] *Discourse at the end of the Synod* (27 October 1990), 5: *L'Osservatore Romano,* 28 October 1990.

4

2.   To remain faithful to the grace received! This gift of God does not cancel human freedom; instead it gives rise to freedom, develops freedom and demands freedom.

For this reason, the total trust in God's unconditional faithfulness to his promise is accompanied in the Church by the grave responsibility to cooperate in the action of God who calls, and to contribute towards creating and preserving the conditions in which the good seed, sown by God, can take root and bring forth abundant fruit. The Church must never cease to pray to the Lord of the harvest that he send labourers into his harvest (cf. *Mt* 9:38). She must propose clearly and courageously to each new generation the vocational call, help people to discern the authenticity of their call from God and to respond to it generously, and give particular care to the formation of candidates for the priesthood.

The formation of future priests, both diocesan and religious, and life-long assiduous care for their personal sanctification in the ministry and for the constant updating of their pastoral commitment are considered by the Church one of the most demanding and important tasks for the future of the evangelization of humanity.

The Church's work of formation is a continuation in time of Christ's own work, which the Evangelist Mark illustrates in these words: "And he went up on the mountain, and called to him those whom he desired; and they came to him. And he appointed twelve, to be with him, and to be sent out to preach and have authority to cast out demons" (*Mk* 3:13-15).

It can be said that through her work of forming candidates to the priesthood and priests themselves, the Church throughout her history has continued to live this passage of the Gospel in various ways and with varying intensity. Today, however, the Church feels called to re-live with a renewed commitment all that the Master did with his Apostles, urged on as she is by the deep and rapid transformations in the societies and culture of our age, by the multiplicity and diversity of contexts in which she announces the Gospel and witnesses to it, by the promising number of priestly vocations being seen in some Dioceses around the world, by the urgency of a new look at the contents and methods of priestly formation, by the concern of Bishops and their communities about a persisting scarcity of clergy, and by the absolute necessity that the "new evangelization" have priests as its initial "new evangelizers".

It is precisely in this cultural and historical context that the last Ordinary General Assembly of the Synod of Bishops took place. Dedicated to "the formation of priests in circumstances of the present day", its purpose was to put into practice the Council's teaching on this matter, making it more up-to-date and incisive in present circumstances, twenty-five years after the Council itself.[3]

---

[3] Cf. *Propositio* 1.

3.　　Following the texts of the Second Vatican Council regarding the ministry of priests and their formation,[4] and with the intention of applying to various situations their rich and authoritative teaching, the Church has on various occasions dealt with the subject of the life, ministry and formation of priests.

She has done this in a more solemn way during the Synods of Bishops. Already in October, 1967, the First General Ordinary Assembly of the Synod devoted five general congregations to the subject of the renewal of seminaries. This work gave a decisive impulse to the formulation of the document of the Congregation for Catholic Education entitled, "Fundamental Norms for Priestly Formation".[5]

The Second Ordinary General Assembly held in 1971 spent half its time on the ministerial priesthood. The fruit of the lengthy synodal discussion, incorporated and condensed in some "recommendations", which were submitted to my predecessor Pope Paul VI and read at the opening of the 1974 Synod, referred principally to the teaching on the ministerial priesthood and to some aspects of priestly spirituality and ministry.

On many other occasions the Church's Magisterium has shown its concern for the life and ministry of priests. It may be said that in the years

---

[4] Cf. Dogmatic Constitution on the Church *Lumen Gentium*, 28; Decree on the Ministry and Life of Priests *Presbyterorum Ordinis;* Decree on Priestly Formation *Optatam Totius.*

[5] *Ratio Fundamentalis Institutionis Sacerdotalis* (6 January 1970): *AAS* 62 (1970), 321-384.

since the Council there has not been any subject treated by the Magisterium which has not in some way, explicitly or implicitly, had to do with the presence of priests in the community as well as their role and the need for them in the life of the Church and the world.

In recent years some have voiced a need to return to the theme of the priesthood, treating it from a relatively new point of view, one that was more adapted to present ecclesial and cultural circumstances. Attention has shifted from the question of the priest's identity to that connected with the process of formation for the priesthood and the quality of priestly life. The new generation of those called to the ministerial priesthood display different characteristics in comparison to those of their immediate predecessors. In addition, they live in a world which in many respects is new and undergoing rapid and continual evolution. All of this cannot be ignored when it comes to programming and carrying out the various phases of formation for those approaching the ministerial priesthood.

Moreover, priests who have been actively involved in the ministry for a more or less lengthy period of time seem to be suffering today from an excessive loss of energy in their ever increasing pastoral activities. Likewise, faced with the difficulties of contemporary culture and society, they feel compelled to re-examine their way of life and their pastoral priorities, and they are more and more aware of their need for ongoing formation.

The concern of the 1990 Synod of Bishops and its discussion focused on the increase of vocations to the priesthood and the formation of candidates in an attempt to help them come to know and follow Jesus, as they prepare to be ordained and to live the Sacrament of Holy Orders, which configures them to Christ the Head and Shepherd, the Servant and Spouse of the Church. At the same time, the Synod searched for forms of ongoing formation to provide realistic and effective means of support for priests in their spiritual life and ministry.

This same Synod also sought to answer a request which was made at the previous Synod on the vocation and mission of the laity in the Church and in the world. Lay people themselves had asked that priests commit themselves to their formation so that they, the laity, could be suitably helped to fulfil their role in the ecclesial mission which is shared by all. Indeed, "the more the lay apostolate develops, the more strongly is perceived the need to have well-formed holy priests. Thus the very life of the People of God manifests the teaching of the Second Vatican Council concerning the relationship between the common priesthood and the ministerial or hierarchical priesthood. For within the mystery of the Church the hierarchy has a ministerial character (cf. *Lumen Gentium*, 10). The more the laity's own sense of vocation is deepened, the more what is proper to the priest stands out".[6]

---

[6] *Discourse at the end of the Synod* (27 October 1990), 3: *loc. cit.*

4.   In the ecclesial experience that is typical of the Synod (that is, "a unique experience on a universal basis of episcopal communion, which strengthens the sense of the universal Church and the sense of responsibility of the Bishops towards the universal Church and her mission, in affective and effective communion around Peter"),[7] *the voice of the various particular Churches*—and in this Synod, for the first time, the voices of some Churches from the East—were clearly heard and taken to heart. The Churches have proclaimed their faith in the fulfilment of God's promise: "I will give you shepherds after my own heart" (*Jer* 3:15), and they have renewed their pastoral commitment to care for vocations and for the formation of priests, aware that on this depends the future of the Church, her development and her universal mission of salvation.

In this Post-Synodal Apostolic Exhortation, I take up anew the rich legacy resulting from the reflections, endeavours and indications which were made during the Synod's preparation, as well as those which accompanied the work of the Synod Fathers, and as the Bishop of Rome and Successor of Peter I add my voice to theirs, addressing it to each and every one of the faithful, and in particular to each priest and to those involved in the important yet demanding ministry of their formation. Yes, in this Exhortation I wish to meet with *each and every priest,* whether diocesan or religious.

[7] *Ibid.,* 1: *loc. cit.*

10

Quoting from the "Final Message of the Synod to the People of God", I make my own the words and the sentiments expressed by the Synod Fathers: "Brother Priests, we want to express our appreciation to you, who are our most important collaborators in the apostolate. Your priesthood is absolutely vital. There is no substitute for it. You carry the main burden of priestly ministry through your day-to-day service of the faithful. You are ministers of the Eucharist and ministers of God's mercy in the Sacrament of Penance. It is you who bring comfort to people and guide them in difficult moments in their lives.

"We acknowledge your work and thank you once again, urging you to continue on your chosen path willingly and joyfully. No one should be discouraged as we are doing God's work; the same God who calls us, sends us and remains with us every day of our lives. We are ambassadors of Christ".[8]

[8] *Message* of the Synod Fathers to the People of God, III: *L'Osservatore Romano,* 29-30 October 1990.

CHAPTER I

CHOSEN FROM AMONG MEN

THE CHALLENGES FACING PRIESTLY FORMATION AT THE CONCLUSION OF THE SECOND MILLENNIUM

THE PRIEST IN HIS TIME

5.   "Every high priest chosen from among men is appointed to act on behalf of men in relation to God" (*Heb* 5:1).

The Letter to the Hebrews clearly affirms the *"human character"* of God's minister: he comes from the human community and is at its service, imitating Jesus Christ "who in every respect has been tempted as we are, yet without sin" (*Heb* 4:15).

God always calls his priests from specific human and ecclesial contexts, which inevitably influence them; and to these same contexts the priest is sent for the service of Christ's Gospel.

For this reason the Synod desired to "contextualize" the subject of priests, viewing it in terms of today's society and today's Church in preparation for the third millennium. This is indicated in the second part of the topic's formulation:

"The formation of priests *in the circumstances of the present day*".

Certainly "there is an essential aspect of the priest that does not change: the priest of tomorrow, no less than the priest of today, must resemble Christ. When Jesus lived on this earth, he manifested in himself the definitive role of the priest, by establishing a ministerial priesthood, with which the Apostles were the first to be invested. This priesthood is destined to last in endless succession throughout history. In this sense the priest of the third millennium will continue the work of the priests who, in the preceding millennia, have animated the life of the Church. In the third millennium the priestly vocation will continue to be the call to live the unique and permanent priesthood of Christ".[9] It is equally certain that the life and ministry of the priest must also "adapt to every era and circumstance of life ... For our part we must therefore seek to be as open as possible to light from on high from the Holy Spirit, in order to discover the tendencies of contemporary society, recognize the deepest spiritual needs, determine the most important concrete tasks and the pastoral methods to adopt, and thus respond adequately to human expectations".[10]

With the duty of bringing together the permanent truth of the priestly ministry and the characteristic requirements of the present day, the Synod Fathers sought to respond to *a few necessary ques-*

---

[9] *Angelus* (14 January 1990), 2: *L'Osservatore Romano*, 15-16 January 1990.
[10] *Ibid.*, 3: *loc. cit.*

tions: What are the positive and negative elements in socio-cultural and ecclesial contexts which affect boys, adolescents and young men who throughout their lives are called to bring to maturity a project of priestly life? What difficulties are posed by our times, and what new possibilities are offered for the exercise of a priestly ministry which corresponds to the gift received in the Sacrament and the demands of the spiritual life which is consistent with it?

I now mention some elements taken from the Synod Fathers' analysis of the situation, fully aware that the great variety of socio-cultural and ecclesial circumstances in different countries limits by necessity our treatment to only the most evident and widespread phenomena, particularly to those which relate to the question of education and priestly formation.

THE GOSPEL TODAY: HOPES AND OBSTACLES

6.   A number of factors seem to be working towards making people today more deeply aware of the dignity of the human person and more open to religious values, to the Gospel and to the priestly ministry.

Despite many contradictions, society is increasingly witnessing a powerful thirst for justice and peace, a more lively sense that humanity must care for creation and respect nature, a more open search for truth, a greater effort to safeguard human dignity, a growing commitment in many sectors of the world population to a more specific international solidarity and a new ordering of the world in freedom and justice. Parallel to the continued development of the potential offered by science and technology and the exchange of information and interaction of cultures, there is a new call for ethics, that is, a quest for meaning, and therefore for an objective standard of values which will delineate the possibilities and limits of progress.

In the more specifically religious and Christian sphere, ideological prejudices and the violent rejection of the message of spiritual and religious values are crumbling and there are arising new and unexpected possibilities of evangelization and the rebirth of ecclesial life in many parts of the world. These are evident in an increased love of the Sacred Scriptures; in the vitality and growing vigour of many young Churches and their ever larger role in the defence and promotion of the values of human life and the person; and in the splendid witness of martyrdom provided by the Churches of Central and Eastern Europe as well as that of the faithfulness and courage of other Churches which are still forced to undergo persecution and tribulation for the faith.[11]

The thirst for God and for an active meaningful relationship with him is so strong today that, where there is a lack of a genuine and full proclamation of the Gospel of Christ, there is a rising spread of forms of religiosity without God and the proliferation of many sects. For all children of the Church, and for priests especially, the increase of

[11] Cf. *Propositio* 3.

these phenomena, even in some traditionally Christian environments, is not only a constant motive to examine our consciences as to the credibility of our witness to the Gospel but at the same time is a sign of how deep and widespread is the search for God.

7.   Mingled with these and other positive factors, there are also, however, many problematic or negative elements.

Rationalism is still very widespread and, in the name of a reductive concept of "science", it renders human reason insensitive to an encounter with Revelation and with divine transcendence.

We should take note also of a desperate defence of personal *subjectivity* which tends to close it off in individualism, rendering it incapable of true human relationships. As a result, many, especially children and young people, seek to compensate for this loneliness with substitutes of various kinds, in more or less acute forms of hedonism or flight from responsibility. Prisoners of the fleeting moment, they seek to "consume" the strongest and most gratifying individual experiences at the level of immediate emotions and sensations, inevitably finding themselves indifferent and "paralyzed" as it were when they come face to face with the summons to embark upon a life project which includes a spiritual and religious dimension and a commitment to solidarity.

Furthermore, despite the fall of ideologies which had made materialism a dogma and the refusal of religion a programme, there is spreading in every part of the world a sort of *practical and existential atheism* which coincides with a secularist outlook on life and human destiny. The individual, "all bound up in himself, this man who makes himself not only the centre of his every interest, but dares to propose himself as the principle and reason of all reality",[12] finds himself ever more bereft of that "supplement of soul" which is all the more necessary to him in proportion as a wide availability of material goods and resources deceives him about his self-sufficiency. There is no longer a need to fight against God; the individual feels he is simply able to do without him.

In this context special mention should be made of *the break-up of the family and an obscuring or distorting of the true meaning of human sexuality.* These phenomena have a very negative effect on the education of young people and on their openness to any kind of religious vocation. Furthermore, one should mention the worsening of social injustices and the concentration of wealth in the hands of a few, the fruit of an inhuman capitalism[13] which increasingly widens the gap between affluent and indigent peoples. In this way tension and unrest are introduced into everyday life, deeply disturbing the lives of people and of whole communities.

There are also worrying and negative factors within the Church herself which have a direct influence on the lives and ministry of priests. For

[12] PAUL VI, *Homily at the 9th Session of the Second Vatican Ecumenical Council* (7 December 1965): *AAS* 58 (1966), 55.
[13] Cf. *Propositio* 3.

example: the lack of due knowledge of the faith among many believers; a catechesis which has little practical effect, stifled as it is by the mass-media whose messages are more widespread and persuasive; an incorrectly understood pluralism in theology, culture and pastoral teaching which, though starting out at times with good intentions, ends up by hindering ecumenical dialogue and threatening the necessary unity of faith; a persistent diffidence towards and almost unacceptance of the Magisterium of the hierarchy; the one-sided tendencies which reduce the richness of the Gospel message and transform the proclamation and witness to the faith into an element of exclusively human and social liberation or into an alienating flight into superstition and religiosity without God.[14]

A particularly important phenomenon, even though it is relatively recent in many traditionally Christian countries, is the presence within the same territory of large concentrations of people of different races and religions, thereby resulting in multi-racial and multi-religious societies. While on the one hand this can be an opportunity for a more frequent and fruitful exercise of dialogue, open-mindedness, good relations and a just tolerance, on the other hand the situation can also result in confusion and relativism, above all among people and populations whose faith has not matured.

Added to these factors, and closely linked with the growth of individualism, is the phenome-

---

[14] Cf. *ibid.*

non of *subjectivism in matters of faith.* An increasing number of Christians seem to have a reduced sensitivity to the universality and objectivity of the doctrine of the faith, because they are subjectively attached to what pleases them, to what corresponds to their own experience, and to what does not impinge on their own habits. In such a context, even the appeal to the inviolability of the individual conscience, in itself a legitimate appeal, may be dangerously marked by ambiguity.

This situation also gives rise to the phenomenon of *belonging to the Church* in ways which are ever more partial and conditional, with a resulting negative influence on the birth of new vocations to the priesthood, on the priest's own self-awareness and on his ministry within the community.

Finally, in many parts of the Church today it is still the scarcity of priests which creates the most serious problem. The faithful are often left to themselves for long periods, without sufficient pastoral support. As a result their growth as Christians suffers, not to mention their capacity to become better promoters of evangelization.

Young people: vocation and priestly formation

8.   The many contradictions and potentialities marking our societies and cultures, as well as ecclesial communities, are perceived, lived and experienced by our young people with a particular intensity and have immediate and very acute repercussions on their personal growth. Thus, the

19

emergence and development of priestly vocations among boys, adolescents and young men are continually under pressure and facing obstacles.

The lure of the so-called "consumer society" is so strong among young people that they become totally dominated and imprisoned by an individualistic, materialistic and hedonistic interpretation of human existence. Material "well-being", which is so intensely sought after, becomes the one ideal to be striven for in life, a well-being which is to be attained in any way and at any price. There is a refusal of anything that speaks of sacrifice and a rejection of any effort to look for and to practise spiritual and religious values. The all-determining "concern" for *having* supplants the primacy of *being,* and consequently personal and interpersonal values are interpreted and lived not according to the logic of giving and generosity but according to the logic of selfish possession and the exploitation of others.

This is particularly reflected in that *outlook on human sexuality* according to which sexuality's dignity in service to communion and to the reciprocal donation between persons becomes degraded and thereby reduced to nothing more than a consumer good. In this case, many young people undergo an affective experience which, instead of contributing to an harmonious and joyous growth in personality which opens them outwards in an act of self-giving, becomes a serious psychological and ethical process of turning inward towards self, a situation which cannot fail to have grave consequences on them in the future.

In the case of some young people a *distorted sense of freedom* lies at the root of these tendencies. Instead of being understood as obedience to objective and universal truth, freedom is lived out as a blind acquiescence to instinctive forces and to an individual's will to power. Therefore, on the level of thought and behaviour, it is almost natural to find an erosion of internal consent to ethical principles. On the religious level, such a situation, if it does not always lead to an explicit refusal of God, causes widespread indifference and results in a life which, even in its more significant moments and more decisive choices, is lived as if God did not exist. In this context it is difficult not only to respond fully to a vocation to the priesthood but even to understand its very meaning as a special witness to the primacy of "being" over "having", and as a recognition that the significance of life consists in a free and responsible giving of oneself to others, a willingness to place oneself entirely at the service of the Gospel and the Kingdom of God as a priest.

Often the world of young people is a "problem" in the Church community itself. In fact, if in them—more so than in adults—there is present a strong tendency to subjectivize the Christian faith and to belong only partially and conditionally to the life and mission of the Church, and if the Church community is slow for a variety of reasons to initiate and sustain an up-to-date and courageous pastoral care for young people, they risk being left to themselves, at the mercy of their psychological frailty, dissatisfied and critical of a world of adults who, in failing to live the faith in a consistent and mature fashion, do not appear to them as credible models.

Thus we see how difficult it is to present young people with a full and penetrating experience of Christian and ecclesial life and to educate them in it. So, the prospect of having a vocation to the priesthood is far from the actual everyday interests which young men have in life.

9.   Nevertheless, there are positive situations and tendencies which bring about and nurture in the heart of adolescents and young men a new readiness, and even a genuine search, for ethical and spiritual values. These naturally offer favourable conditions for embarking on the journey of a vocation which leads towards the total gift of self to Christ and to the Church in the priesthood.

First of all, mention should be made of the decrease of certain phenomena which had caused many problems in the recent past, such as radical rebellion, libertarian tendencies, utopian claims, indiscriminate forms of socialization and violence.

It must be recognized, moreover, that today's young people, with the vigour and vitality typical of their age, are also bearers of ideals which are coming to the fore in history: the thirst for freedom, the recognition of the inestimable value of the person, the need for authenticity and sincerity, a new conception and style of reciprocity in the rapport between men and women, a convinced and earnest seeking after a more just, sympathetic and united world, openness and dialogue with all, and the commitment to peace.

The fruitful and active development among so many young people today of numerous and varied forms of voluntary service, directed towards the most forgotten and forsaken of our society, represents in these times a particularly important resource for personal growth. It stimulates and sustains young people in a style of life which is less self-interested and more open and sympathetic towards the poor. This way of life can help young men perceive, desire and accept a vocation to stable and total service of others, following the path of complete consecration to God as a priest.

The recent collapse of ideologies, the heavily critical opposition to a world of adults who do not always offer a witness of a life based on moral and transcendent values, and the experience of companions who seek escape through drugs and violence, contribute in no small fashion to making more keen and inescapable the fundamental question as to what values are truly capable of giving the fullest meaning to life, suffering and death. For many young people the question of religion and the need for spirituality are becoming more explicit. This is illustrated in the desire for "desert experiences" and for prayer, in the return to a more personal and regular reading of the Word of God and in the study of theology.

As has happened in their involvement in the sphere of voluntary social service, young people are becoming more actively involved as leaders in the ecclesial community, above all through their membership of various groups, whether traditional but renewed ones or of more recent origin. Their experience of a Church challenged to undertake a "new evangelization" by virtue of her faithfulness to the Spirit who animates her and in response to the demands of a world far from Christ but in need of him, as well as their experience of a Church ever more united with individuals and peoples in the defence and promotion of the dignity of the person and of the human rights of each and every one — these experiences open the hearts and lives of the young to the exciting and demanding ideals which can find their concrete fulfilment in following Christ and in embracing the priesthood.

Naturally it is not possible to ignore this human and ecclesial situation, characterized by strong ambivalences, not only in the pastoral care of vocations and the formation of future priests, but also in the care of priests in their life and ministry and their ongoing formation. At the same time, while it is possible to detect various forms of "crisis" to which priests are subjected today in their ministry, in their spiritual life and indeed in the very interpretation of the nature and significance of the ministerial priesthood, mention must likewise be made, in a spirit of joy and hope, of the new positive possibilities which the present historical moment is offering to priests for the fulfilment of their mission.

10.   The complex situation of the present day, briefly outlined above in general terms and examples, needs not only to be known but also and above all to be interpreted. Only in this way can an adequate answer be given to the fundamental question: How can we form priests who are truly able to respond to the demands of our times and capable of evangelizing the world of today? [15]

Knowledge of the situation is important. However, simply to provide data is not enough; what is needed is a "scientific" inquiry in order to sketch a precise and concrete picture of today's socio-cultural and ecclesial circumstances.

Even more important is an *interpretation* of the situation. Such an interpretation is required because of the ambivalence, and at times contradictions, which are characteristic of the present situation where there is an mixture of difficulties and potentialities, negative elements and reasons for hope, obstacles and alternatives, as in the field mentioned in the Gospel where good seed and weeds are both sown and "co-exist" (cf. *Mt* 13:24ff).

It is not always easy to give an interpretive reading capable of distinguishing good from evil or signs of hope from threats. In the formation of priests it is not sufficient simply to welcome the positive factors and to counteract the negative ones. The positive factors themselves need to be

---

[15] Cf. SYNOD OF BISHOPS, "The Formation of Priests in the Circumstances of the Present Day" — *Lineamenta,* 5-6.

subjected to a careful work of discernment, so that they do not become isolated and contradict one another, becoming absolutes and at odds with one another. The same is true for the negative factors, which are not to be rejected *en bloc* and without distinction, because in each one there may lie hidden some value which awaits liberation and restoration to its full truth.

For a believer the interpretation of the historical situation finds its principle for understanding and its criterion for making practical choices in a new and unique reality, that is, in a *Gospel discernment*. This interpretation is a work which is done in the light and strength provided by the true and living Gospel, which is Jesus Christ, and in virtue of the gift of the Holy Spirit. In such a way, Gospel discernment gathers from the historical situation, from its events and circumstances, not just a simple "fact" to be precisely recorded yet capable of leaving a person indifferent or passive, but a "task", a challenge to responsible freedom, both of the individual person and of the community. It is a "challenge" which is linked to a "call" which God causes to sound in the historical situation itself. In this situation, and also through it, God calls the believer, and first of all the Church, to ensure that "the Gospel of vocation and priesthood" expresses its perennial truth in the changing circumstances of life. In this case, the words of the Second Vatican Council are also applicable to the formation of priests: "The Church has always had the duty of scrutinizing the signs of the times and of interpreting them in the light of the Gospel, so that in a language intelligible to every generation, she can respond to the perennial questions which people ask about this present life and the life to come, and about the relationship of the one to the other. We must therefore recognize and understand the world in which we live, its expectations, its longings, and its often dramatic characteristics".[16]

This Gospel discernment is based on trust in the love of Jesus Christ, who always and tirelessly cares for his Church (cf. *Eph* 5:29), he the Lord and Master, the Key, the Centre and the Purpose of the whole of man's history.[17] This discernment is nourished by the light and strength of the Holy Spirit, who evokes everywhere and in all circumstances obedience to the faith, the joyous courage of following Jesus and the gift of wisdom, which judges all things and is judged by no one (cf. *1 Cor* 2:15). It rests on the fidelity of the Father to his promises.

In this way the Church feels that she can face the difficulties and challenges of this new period of history and can also provide, in the present and in the future, priests who are well trained to be convinced and fervent ministers of the "new evangelization", faithful and generous servants of Jesus Christ and of the human family. We are not unmindful of difficulties in this regard; they are

[16] Pastoral Constitution on the Church in the Modern World *Gaudium et Spes,* 4.
[17] Cf. SYNOD OF BISHOPS, 7th Ordinary General Assembly, *Final Message of the Synod Fathers to the People of God* (28 October 1990), I: *loc. cit.*

27

neither few nor insignificant. However, to sur-
mount these difficulties we have at our disposal
our hope, our faith in the unfailing love of Christ,
and our certainty that the priestly ministry in
the life of the Church and in the world knows
no substitute.

CHAPTER II

HE HAS ANOINTED ME
AND HAS SENT ME FORTH

THE NATURE AND MISSION
OF THE MINISTERIAL PRIESTHOOD

A LOOK AT THE PRIEST

11.   "The eyes of all in the synagogue were
fixed on him" (*Lk* 4:20). What the Evangelist
Luke says about the people in the synagogue at
Nazareth that sabbath, listening to Jesus' com-
mentary on the words of the Prophet Isaiah which
he had just read, can be applied to all Christians.
They are always called to recognize in Jesus of
Nazareth the definitive fulfilment of the message
of the Prophets: "And he began to say to them,
'Today this Scripture has been fulfilled in your
hearing'" (*Lk* 4:21). The "Scripture" he had read
was this: "The Spirit of the Lord is upon me,
because he has anointed me to preach good news
to the poor. He has sent me to proclaim release to
the captives and recovering of sight to the blind,
to set at liberty those who are oppressed, to proclaim the acceptable year of the Lord" (*Lk* 4:18-
19; cf. *Is* 61:1-2). Jesus thus presents himself as
filled with the Spirit, "consecrated with an anointing", "sent to preach good news to the poor". He

29

is the Messiah, the Messiah who is Priest, Prophet and King.

These are the features of Christ upon which the eyes of faith and love of Christians should be fixed. Using this "contemplation" as a starting-point and making continual reference to it, the Synod Fathers reflected on the problem of priestly formation in present-day circumstances. This problem cannot be solved without previous reflection upon the goal of formation, that is, the ministerial priesthood, or, more precisely, the ministerial priesthood as a participation, in the Church, in the very priesthood of Jesus Christ. Knowledge of the nature and mission of the ministerial priesthood is an essential presupposition, and at the same time the surest guide and incentive towards the development of pastoral activities in the Church for fostering and discerning vocations to the priesthood and training those called to the ordained ministry.

A correct and in-depth awareness of the nature and mission of the ministerial priesthood is the path which must be taken—and in fact the Synod did take it—in order to emerge from the crisis *of priestly identity*. In the Final Address to the Synod I stated: "This crisis arose in the years immediately following the Council. It was based on an erroneous understanding of—and sometimes even a conscious bias against—the doctrine of the Conciliar Magisterium. Undoubtedly, herein lies one of the reasons for the great number of defections experienced then by the Church, losses which did serious harm to pastoral

ministry and priestly vocations, especially missionary vocations. It is as though the 1990 Synod, re-
discovering by means of the many statements
which we heard in this hall, the full depth of
priestly identity, has striven to instil hope in the
wake of these sad losses. These statements showed
an awareness of the specific ontological bond
which unites the priesthood to Christ the High
Priest and Good Shepherd. This identity is built
upon the type of formation which must be provided for priesthood, and then endure throughout
the priest's whole life. This was the precise purpose of the Synod".[18]

For this reason the Synod considered it necessary to summarize the nature and mission of the
ministerial priesthood, as the Church's faith has
acknowledged them down the centuries of its history and as the Second Vatican Council has presented them anew to the people of our day.[19]

IN THE CHURCH AS MYSTERY, COMMUNION AND MISSION

12.   "The priest's identity," as the Synod
Fathers wrote, "like every Christian identity, has

---

[18] *Discourse at the end of the Synod* (27 October 1990), 4: *loc. cit.;*
cf. *Letter to Priests for Holy Thursday 1991* (10 March 1991): *L'Osservatore Romano,* 15 March 1991.
[19] Cf. Dogmatic Constitution on the Church *Lumen Gentium*; Decree on the Ministry and Life of Priests *Presbyterorum Ordinis*; Decree
on Priestly Formation *Optatam Totius*; SACRED CONGREGATION FOR
CATHOLIC EDUCATION, *Ratio Fundamentalis Institutionis Sacerdotalis*
(6 January 1970): *loc. cit.,* 321-384; SYNOD OF BISHOPS, 2nd Ordinary General Assembly, 1971.

31

its source in the Blessed Trinity",[20] which is revealed and is communicated to people in Christ, establishing, in him and through the Spirit, the Church as "the seed and the beginning of the Kingdom".[21] The Apostolic Exhortation *Christifideles Laici,* summarizing the Council's teaching, presents the Church as mystery, communion and mission: "She is mystery because the very life and love of the Father, Son and Holy Spirit are the gift gratuitously offered to all those who are born of water and the Spirit (cf. *Jn* 3.5), and called to re-live the very *communion* of God and to manifest it and communicate it in history (mission)".[22]

It is within the Church's mystery, as a mystery of Trinitarian communion in missionary tension, that every Christian identity is revealed, and likewise the specific identity of the priest and his ministry. Indeed, the priest, by virtue of the consecration which he receives in the Sacrament of Orders, is sent forth by the Father through the mediatorship of Jesus Christ, to whom he is configured in a special way as Head and Shepherd of his people, in order to live and work by the power of the Holy Spirit in service of the Church and for the salvation of the world.[23]

In this way the fundamentally "relational" dimension of priestly identity can be understood.

---

[20] *Propositio* 7.
[21] SECOND VATICAN ECUMENICAL COUNCIL, Dogmatic Constitution on the Church *Lumen Gentium,* 5.
[22] Post-Synodal Apostolic Exhortation *Christifideles Laici* (30 December 1988), 8: *AAS* 81 (1989), 405; cf. SYNOD OF BISHOPS, 2nd Extraordinary General Assembly, 1985.
[23] Cf. *Propositio* 7.

Through the priesthood which arises from the depths of the ineffable mystery of God, that is, from the love of the Father, the grace of Jesus Christ and the Holy Spirit's gift of unity, the priest sacramentally enters into communion with the Bishop and with other priests,[24] in order to serve the People of God who are the Church and to draw all mankind to Christ in accordance with the Lord's prayer: "Holy Father, keep them in your name, which you have given me, that they may be one, even as we are one ... even as you, Father, are in me, and I in you, that they also may be in us, so that the world may believe that you have sent me" (*Jn* 17:11, 21).

Consequently, the nature and mission of the ministerial priesthood cannot be defined except through this multiple and rich interconnection of relationships which arise from the Blessed Trinity and are prolonged in the communion of the Church, as a sign and instrument of Christ, of communion with God and of the unity of all humanity.[25] In this context the ecclesiology of communion becomes decisive for understanding the identity of the priest, his essential dignity, and his vocation and mission among the People of God and in the world. Reference to the Church is therefore necessary, even if it is not primary, in defining the identity of the priest. As a *mystery, the Church is essentially related to Jesus Christ.* She is

---

[24] Cf. SECOND VATICAN ECUMENICAL COUNCIL, Decree on the Ministry and Life of Priests *Presbyterorum Ordinis,* 7-8.

[25] Cf. SECOND VATICAN ECUMENICAL COUNCIL, Dogmatic Constitution on the Church *Lumen Gentium,* 1.

his fullness, his body, his spouse. She is the "sign" and living "memorial" of his permanent presence and activity in our midst and on our behalf. The priest finds the full truth of his identity in being a derivation, a specific participation in and continuation of Christ himself, the one High Priest of the new and eternal Covenant. The priest is a living and transparent image of Christ the Priest. The priesthood of Christ, the expression of his absolute "newness" in salvation history, constitutes the one source and essential model of the priesthood shared by all Christians and the priest in particular. Reference to Christ is thus the absolutely necessary key for understanding the reality of priesthood.

THE FUNDAMENTAL RELATIONSHIP WITH CHRIST THE HEAD AND SHEPHERD

13.   Jesus Christ has revealed in himself the perfect and definitive features of the priesthood of the new Covenant.[26] He did this throughout his earthly life, but especially in the central event of his Passion, Death and Resurrection.

As the author of the Letter to the Hebrews writes, Jesus, being a man like us and at the same time the only begotten Son of God, is in his very being the perfect mediator between the Father and humanity (cf. *Heb* 8-9). Thanks to the gift of his Holy Spirit he gives us immediate access to God: "God has sent the Spirit of his Son into

[26] Cf. *Propositio* 7.

our hearts, crying, 'Abba! Father!'" (*Gal* 4:6; cf. *Rom* 8:15).

Jesus brought his role as mediator to complete fulfilment when he offered himself on the Cross, thereby opening to us, once and for all, access to the heavenly sanctuary, to the Father's house (cf. *Heb* 9:24-28). Compared with Jesus, Moses and all other "mediators" between God and his people in the Old Testament—kings, priests and prophets—are no more than "figures" and "shadows of the good things to come" instead of "the true form of these realities" (cf. *Heb* 10:1).

Jesus is the promised Good Shepherd (cf. *Ez* 34), who knows each one of his sheep, who offers his life for them and who wishes to gather them together as one flock with one shepherd (cf. *Jn* 10:11-16). He is the Shepherd who has come "not to be served but to serve" (*Mt* 20:28), who in the Paschal action of the washing of the feet (cf. *Jn* 13:1-20) leaves to his disciples a model of service to one another and who freely offers himself as the "innocent lamb" sacrificed for our redemption (cf. *Jn* 1:36; *Rev* 5:6, 12).

With the one definitive sacrifice of the Cross, Jesus communicated to all his disciples the dignity and mission of priests of the new and eternal Covenant. And thus the promise which God had made to Israel was fulfilled: "You shall be to me a kingdom of priests and a holy nation" (*Ex* 19:6). According to Saint Peter, the whole people of the New Covenant is established as "a spiritual house", "a holy priesthood, to offer spiritual sacrifices acceptable to God through Jesus Christ"

(*1 Pt* 2:5). The baptized are "living stones" who build the spiritual edifice by keeping close to Christ, "that living stone ... in God's sight chosen and precious" (*1 Pt* 2:4). The new priestly people which is the Church not only has its authentic image in Christ, but also receives from him a real ontological share in his one eternal priesthood, to which she must conform every aspect of her life.

14. For the sake of this universal priesthood of the New Covenant Jesus gathered disciples during his earthly mission (cf. *Lk* 10:1-12) and with a specific and authoritative mandate he called and appointed the Twelve "to be with him, and to be sent out to preach and have authority to cast out demons" (*Mk* 3:14-15).

For this reason, already during his public ministry (cf. *Mt* 16: 18), and then most fully after his Death and Resurrection (cf. *Mt* 28; *Jn* 20; 21), Jesus had conferred on Peter and the Twelve entirely special powers with regard to the future community and the evangelization of all peoples. After having called them to follow him, he kept them at his side and lived with them, imparting his teaching of salvation to them through word and example, and finally he sent them out to all mankind. To enable them to carry out this mission Jesus confers upon the Apostles, by a specific Paschal outpouring of the Holy Spirit, the same messianic authority which he had received from the Father, conferred in its fullness in his Resurrection: "All authority in heaven and on earth has been given to me. Go therefore and make disciples of all nations, baptizing them in the name of the Father and of the Son and of the Holy Spirit, teaching them to observe all that I have commanded you; and lo, I am with you always, to the close of the age" (*Mt* 28:18-20).

Jesus thus established a close relationship between the ministry entrusted to the Apostles and his own mission: "He who receives you receives me, and he who receives me receives him who sent me" (*Mt* 10:40); "He who hears you hears me, and he who rejects you rejects me, and he who rejects me rejects him who sent me" (*Lk* 10:16). Indeed, in the light of the Paschal event of the Death and Resurrection, the Fourth Gospel affirms this with great force and clarity: "As the Father has sent me, even so I send you" (*Jn* 20:21; cf. 13:20; 17:18). Just as Jesus has a mission which comes to him directly from God and makes present the very authority of God (cf. *Mt* 7:29; 21:23; *Mk* 1:27; 11:28; *Lk* 20:2; 24:19), so too the Apostles have a mission which comes to them from Jesus. And just as "the Son can do nothing of his own accord" (*Jn* 5:19) such that his teaching is not his own but the teaching of the One who sent him (cf. *Jn* 7:16), so Jesus says to the Apostles: "apart from me you can do nothing" (*Jn* 15:5). Their mission is not theirs but is the same mission of Jesus. All this is possible not as a result of human abilities, but only with the "gift" of Christ and his Spirit, with the "Sacrament": "Receive the Holy Spirit. If you forgive the sins of any, they are forgiven; if you retain the sins of any, they are retained" (*Jn* 20:22-23). And so the Apostles, not by any special merit of their own, but only through a gratuitous participation in the grace of Christ, prolong throughout history to the end of time the same mission of Jesus on behalf of humanity.

The sign and presupposition of the authenticity and fruitfulness of this mission is the Apostles' unity with Jesus and, in him, with one another and with the Father, as the priestly prayer of our Lord, which sums up his mission, bears witness (cf. *Jn* 17:20-23).

15.   In their turn, the Apostles, appointed by the Lord, progressively carried out their mission by calling, in various but complementary ways, other men as Bishops, as priests and as deacons, in order to fulfil the command of the Risen Jesus who sent them forth to all people in every age.

The writings of the New Testament are unanimous in stressing that it is the same Spirit of Christ who introduces these men chosen from among their brethren into the ministry. Through the laying on of hands (cf. *Acts* 6:6; *1 Tim* 4:14; 5:22; *2 Tim* 1:6) which transmits the gift of the Spirit, they are called and empowered to continue the same ministry of reconciliation, of shepherding the flock of God and of teaching (cf. *Acts* 20:28; *1 Pt* 5:2).

Therefore, priests are called to prolong the presence of Christ, the One High Priest, embodying his way of life and making him visible in the midst of the flock entrusted to their care. We find this clearly and precisely stated in the First Letter of Peter: "I exhort the *elders* among you, as a *fellow elder* and a witness of the sufferings of Christ as well as a partaker in the glory that is to be revealed. Tend the flock of God that is your charge, not by constraint but willingly, not for shameful gain but eagerly, not as domineering over those in your charge but being examples to the flock. And when the chief Shepherd is manifested you will obtain the unfading crown of glory" (*1 Pt* 5:1-4).

In the Church and on behalf of the Church, priests are a sacramental representation of Jesus Christ, the Head and Shepherd, authoritatively proclaiming his Word, repeating his acts of forgiveness and his offer of salvation, particularly in Baptism, Penance and the Eucharist, showing his loving concern to the point of a total gift of self for the flock, which they gather into unity and lead to the Father through Christ and in the Spirit. In a word, priests exist and act in order to proclaim the Gospel to the world and to build up the Church in the name and person of Christ the Head and Shepherd.[27]

This is the ordinary and proper way in which ordained ministers share in the one priesthood of Christ. By the sacramental anointing of Holy Orders, the Holy Spirit configures them in a new and special way to Jesus Christ the Head and Shepherd; he forms and strengthens them with his pastoral charity; and he gives them an

[27] *Ibid.*

authoritative role in the Church as servants of the proclamation of the Gospel to every people and of the fullness of Christian life of all the baptized.

The truth of the priest as it emerges from the Word of God, that is, from Jesus Christ himself and from his constitutive plan for the Church, is thus proclaimed with joyful gratitude by the Preface of the Liturgy of the Chrism Mass: "By your Holy Spirit you anointed your only Son High Priest of the new and eternal Covenant. With wisdom and love you have planned that this one priesthood should continue in the Church. Christ gives the dignity of a royal priesthood to the people he has made his own. From these, with a brother's love, he chooses men to share his sacred ministry by the laying on of hands. He appointed them to renew in his name the sacrifice of redemption as they set before your family his paschal meal. He calls them to lead your holy people in love, nourish them by your word, and strengthen them through the sacraments. Father, they are to give their lives in your service and for the salvation of your people as they strive to grow in the likeness of Christ and honour you by their courageous witness of faith and love".

SERVING THE CHURCH AND THE WORLD

16.   The priest's fundamental relationship is to Jesus Christ, Head and Shepherd. Indeed, the priest participates in a specific and authoritative way in the "consecration/anointing" and in the

"mission" of Christ (cf. *Lk* 4:18-19). But intimately linked to this relationship is the priest's relationship with the Church. It is not a question of "relations" which are merely juxtaposed, but rather of ones which are interiorly united in a kind of mutual immanence. The priest's relation to the Church is inscribed in the very relation which the priest has to Christ, such that the "sacramental representation" to Christ serves as the basis and inspiration for the relation of the priest to the Church.

In this sense the Synod Fathers wrote: "Inasmuch as he represents Christ the Head, Shepherd and Spouse of the Church, the priest is placed not only *in the Church* but also *in the forefront of the Church*. The priesthood, along with the word of God and the sacramental signs which it serves, belongs to the constitutive elements of the Church. The ministry of the priest is entirely on behalf of the Church; it aims at promoting the exercise of the common priesthood of the entire people of God; it is ordered not only to the particular Church but also to the universal Church (*Presbyterorum Ordinis,* 10), in communion with the Bishop, with Peter and under Peter. Through the priesthood of the Bishop, the priesthood of the second order is incorporated in the apostolic structure of the Church. In this way priests, like the Apostles, act as ambassadors of Christ (cf. *2 Cor* 5:20). This is the basis of the missionary character of every priest".[28]

[28] *Propositio* 7.

Therefore, the ordained ministry arises with the Church and has in Bishops, and in priests who are related to and are in communion with them, a particular relation to the original ministry of the Apostles—to which it truly "succeeds"—even though with regard to the latter it assumes different forms.

Consequently, the ordained priesthood ought not to be thought of as existing prior to the Church, because it is totally at the service of the Church. Nor should it be considered as posterior to the ecclesial community, as if the Church could be imagined as already established without this priesthood.

The relation of the priest to Jesus Christ, and in him to his Church, is found in the very *being* of the priest, by virtue of his sacramental consecration/anointing, and in his *activity,* that is in his mission or ministry. In particular, "the priest minister is the servant of Christ present in the *Church as mystery, communion and mission.* In virtue of his participation in the 'anointing' and 'mission' of Christ, the priest can continue Christ's prayer, word, sacrifice and salvific action in the Church. In this way, the priest is a *servant of the Church as mystery* because he actuates the Church's sacramental signs of the presence of the Risen Christ. He is a *servant of the Church as communion* because—in union with the Bishop and closely related to the presbyterate—he builds up the unity of the Church community in the harmony of diverse vocations, charisms and services. Finally, the priest is a servant to the Church as mission because he makes the community a herald and witness of the Gospel".[29]

Thus, by his very nature and sacramental mission, the priest appears in the structure of the Church as a sign of the absolute priority and gratuitousness of the grace given to the Church by the Risen Christ. Through the ministerial priesthood the Church becomes aware in faith that her being comes not from herself but from the grace of Christ in the Holy Spirit. The Apostles and their successors, inasmuch as they exercise an authority which comes to them from Christ, the Head and Shepherd, are placed—with their ministry—*in the forefront of the Church* as a visible continuation and sacramental sign of Christ in his own position before the Church and the world, as the enduring and ever-new source of salvation, he "who is Head of the Church, his Body, and is himself its Saviour" (*Eph* 5:23).

17.   By its very nature, the ordained ministry can be carried out only to the extent that the priest is united to Christ through sacramental participation in the priestly order, and thus to the extent that he is in hierarchical communion with his own Bishop. The ordained ministry has a radical *"communitarian form"* and can only be carried out as "a collective work".[30] The Council

[29] SYNOD OF BISHOPS, 8th Ordinary General Assembly, "The Formation of Priests in the Circumstances of the Present Day", *Instrumentum Laboris,* 16; cf. *Propositio* 7.

[30] *Angelus* (25 February 1990): *L'Osservatore Romano,* 26-27 February 1990.

dealt extensively with this communal aspect of the nature of the priesthood,[31] examining in succession the relationship of the priest with his own Bishop, with other priests and with the lay faithful.

The ministry of priests is above all communion and a responsible and necessary cooperation with the Bishop's ministry, in concern for the universal Church and for the individual particular Churches, for whose service they form with the Bishop a single presbyterate.

Each priest, whether diocesan or religious, is united to the other members of this presbyterate on the basis of the Sacrament of Holy Orders and by particular bonds of apostolic charity, ministry and fraternity. All priests in fact, whether diocesan or religious, share in the one priesthood of Christ the Head and Shepherd; "they work for the same cause, namely, the building up of the Body of Christ, which demands a variety of functions and new adaptations, especially at the present time",[32] and is enriched down the centuries by ever-new charisms.

Finally, because their role and task within the Church do not replace but promote the baptismal priesthood of the entire people of God, leading it to its full ecclesial realization, priests have a positive and helping relationship to the laity. Priests are there to serve the faith, hope and charity of the laity. They recognize and uphold, as brothers

[31] Cf. Decree on the Ministry and Life of Priests *Presbyterorum Ordinis*, 7-9.
[32] *Ibid.*, 8; cf. *Propositio 7*.

and friends, the dignity of the laity as children of God and help them to exercise fully their specific role in the overall context of the Church's mission.[33] The ministerial priesthood conferred by the Sacrament of Holy Orders and the common or "royal" priesthood of the faithful, which differ essentially and not only in degree,[34] are ordered one to the other, for each in its own way derives from the one priesthood of Christ. Indeed, the ministerial priesthood does not of itself signify a greater degree of holiness with regard to the common priesthood of the faithful; through it, Christ gives to priests, in the Spirit, a particular gift so that they can help the People of God to exercise faithfully and fully the common priesthood which it has received.[35]

18.   As the Council points out, "the spiritual gift which priests have received in ordination does not prepare them merely for a limited and circumscribed mission, but for the fullest, in fact the universal mission of salvation to the end of the earth. The reason is that every priestly ministry shares in the fullness of the mission entrusted by Christ to the Apostles".[36] By the very nature of their ministry they should therefore be penetrated and animated by a profound missionary spirit and "with that

[33] SECOND VATICAN ECUMENICAL COUNCIL, Decree on the Ministry and Life of Priests *Presbyterorum Ordinis,* 9.
[34] Cf. SECOND VATICAN ECUMENICAL COUNCIL, Dogmatic Constitution on the Church *Lumen Gentium,* 10.
[35] Cf. *Propositio* 7.
[36] Decree on the Ministry and Life of Priests *Presbyterorum Ordinis* 10.

truly Catholic spirit which habitually looks beyond the boundaries of diocese, country or rite, to meet the needs of the whole Church, being prepared in spirit to preach the Gospel everywhere".[37]

Furthermore, precisely because within the Church's life the priest is a man of communion, in his relations with all people he must be a man of mission and dialogue. Deeply rooted in the truth and charity of Christ, and impelled by the desire and imperative to proclaim Christ's salvation to all, the priest is called to witness in all his relationships to fraternity, service and a common quest for the truth, as well as a concern for the promotion of justice and peace. This is the case above all with the brethren of other Churches and Christian denominations; but it also extends to the followers of other religions; to people of good will, and in particular to the poor and the defenceless, and to all who yearn, even if they do not know it or cannot express it, for the truth and the salvation of Christ, in accordance with the words of Jesus who said: "Those who are well have no need of a physician, but those who are sick; I came not to call the righteous, but sinners" (*Mk* 2:17).

Today in particular, the pressing pastoral task of the new evangelization calls for the involvement of the entire People of God, and requires a new fervour, new methods and a new expression for the announcing and witnessing of the Gospel. This task demands priests who are deeply and

[37] Decree on Priestly Formation *Optatam Totius,* 20.

fully immersed in the mystery of Christ and capable of embodying a new style of pastoral life, marked by a profound communion with the Pope, the Bishops and other priests, and a fruitful cooperation with the lay faithful, always respecting and fostering the different roles, charisms and ministries present within the ecclesial community.[38]

"Today this scripture has been fulfilled in your hearing" (*Lk* 4:21). Let us listen, once again, to these words of Jesus, in the light of the ministerial priesthood which we have presented in its nature and mission. The "today" to which Jesus refers, precisely because it belongs to and defines the "fullness of time", the time of full and definitive salvation, indicates the time of the Church. The consecration and mission of Christ: "The Spirit of the Lord ... has anointed me and has sent me to preach good news to the poor ..." (cf. *Lk* 4:18), are the living branch from which bud the consecration and mission of the Church, the "fullness" of Christ (cf. *Eph* 1:23). In the rebirth of Baptism the Spirit of the Lord is poured out on all believers, consecrating them as a spiritual temple and a holy priesthood and sending them forth to make known the marvels of him who out of darkness has called them into his marvellous light (cf. *1 Pt* 2:4-10). *The priest shares in Christ's consecration and mission in a specific and authoritative way,* through the Sacrament of Holy Orders, by virtue of which he is configured in his being to Jesus Christ, Head and Shepherd, and shares in the

[38] Cf. *Propositio* 12.

47

mission of "preaching the good news to the poor" in the name and person of Christ himself.

In their Final Message the Synod Fathers summarized briefly but eloquently the "truth", or better the "mystery" and "gift" of the ministerial priesthood, when they stated: "We derive our identity ultimately from the love of the Father, we turn our gaze to the Son, sent by the Father as High Priest and Good Shepherd. Through the power of the Holy Spirit, we are united sacramentally to him in the ministerial priesthood. Our priestly life and activity continue the life and activity of Christ himself. Here lies our identity, our true dignity, the source of our joy, the very basis of our life".[39]

[39] *Final Message of the Synod Fathers to tne People of God* (28 October 1990), III: *loc. cit.*

CHAPTER III

THE SPIRIT OF THE LORD IS UPON ME

THE SPIRITUAL LIFE OF THE PRIEST

A "SPECIFIC" VOCATION TO HOLINESS

19.   "The Spirit of the Lord is upon me" (*Lk* 4:18). The Spirit is not simply "upon" the Messiah, but he "fills" him, penetrating every part of him and reaching to the very depths of all that he is and does. Indeed, the Spirit is the principle of the "consecration" and "mission" of the Messiah: "because he has anointed me, and sent me to preach good news to the poor ..." (cf. *Lk* 4:18). Through the Spirit, Jesus belongs totally and exclusively to God and shares in the infinite holiness of God, who calls him, chooses him and sends him forth. In this way the Spirit of the Lord is revealed as the source of holiness and of the call to holiness.

This same "Spirit of the Lord" is "upon" the entire People of God which becomes established as a People "consecrated" to God and "sent" by God to announce the Gospel of salvation. The members of the People of God are "inebriated" and "sealed" with the Spirit (cf. *1 Cor* 12:13; *2 Cor* 1:21ff; *Eph* 1:13; 4:30) and called to holiness.

49

In particular, *the Spirit reveals to us and communicates the fundamental calling* which the Father addresses to everyone from all eternity: the vocation to be *"holy* and blameless before him ... in love"*, by virtue of our predestination to be his adopted children through Jesus Christ (cf. *Eph* 1:4-5). This is not all. By revealing and communicating this vocation to us, *the Spirit becomes within us the principle and wellspring of its fulfilment.* He, the Spirit of the Son (cf. *Gal* 4:6), configures us to Christ Jesus and makes us sharers in his life as Son, that is, sharers in his life of love for the Father and for our brothers and sisters. "If we live by the Spirit, let us also walk by the Spirit" (*Gal* 5:25). In these words the Apostle Paul reminds us that a Christian life is a "spiritual life", that is, a life enlivened and led by the Spirit towards holiness or the perfection of charity.

The Council's statement that "all Christians in any state or walk of life are called to the fullness of Christian life and to the perfection of charity" [40] applies in a special way to priests. They are called not only because they have been baptized, but also and specifically because they are priests, that is, under a new title and in new and different ways deriving from the Sacrament of Holy Orders.

20.   The Council's Decree on Priestly Life and Ministry gives us a particularly rich and thought-provoking synthesis of the priest's "spiritual life" and of the gift and duty to become "saints": "By

[40] Dogmatic Constitution on the Church *Lumen Gentium*, 40.

the Sacrament of Orders priests are configured to Christ the priest so that as ministers of the Head and co-workers with the episcopal order they may build up and establish his whole Body which is the Church. Like all Christians they have already received in the consecration of Baptism the sign and gift of their great calling and grace which enables and obliges them even in the midst of human weakness to seek perfection (cf. *2 Cor* 12:9), according to the Lord's word: You, therefore, must be perfect, as your heavenly Father is perfect' (*Mt* 5:48). But priests are bound in a special way to strive for this perfection, since they are consecrated to God in a new way by their ordination. They have become living instruments of Christ the eternal priest, so that through the ages they can accomplish his wonderful work of reuniting the whole human race with heavenly power. Therefore, since every priest in his own way represents the person of Christ himself, he is endowed with a special grace. By this grace the priest, through his service of the people committed to his care and all the People of God, is able the better to pursue the perfection of Christ, whose place he takes. The human weakness of his flesh is remedied by the holiness of him who became for us a high priest holy, innocent, undefiled, separated from sinners' (*Heb* 7:26)".[41]

The Council first affirms the *"common" vocation to holiness.* This vocation is rooted in Baptism,

[41] Decree on the Ministry and Life of Priests *Presbyterorum Ordinis,* 12.

which characterizes the priest as one of the "faithful" (*Christifidelis*), as a "brother among brothers", a member of the People of God, joyfully sharing in the gifts of salvation (cf. *Eph* 4:4-6) and in the common duty of walking "according to the Spirit" in the footsteps of the one Master and Lord. We recall the celebrated words of Saint Augustine: "For you I am a Bishop, with you I am a Christian. The former title speaks of a task undertaken, the latter of grace; the former betokens danger, the latter salvation".[42]

With the same clarity the conciliar text also speaks of a *"specific" vocation to holiness,* or more precisely of a vocation based on the Sacrament of Holy Orders, as a sacrament proper and specific to the priest, and thus involving a new consecration to God through ordination. Saint Augustine also alludes to this specific vocation when, after the words "For you I am a Bishop, with you I am a Christian", he goes on to say: "If therefore it is to me a greater cause for joy to have been rescued with you than to have been placed as your leader, following the Lord's command, I will devote myself to the best of my abilities to serve you, so as not to show myself ungrateful to him who rescued me with that price which has made me your fellow servant".[43]

The conciliar text goes on to point out some elements necessary for defining what constitutes the "specific quality" of the priest's spiritual life.

---

[42] *Sermo 340*, 1: PL 38:1483.
[43] *Ibid., loc. cit.*

These are elements connected with the priest's "consecration", which configures him to Christ the Head and Shepherd of the Church, with the "mission" or ministry peculiar to the priest, which equips and obliges him to be a "living instrument of Christ the eternal priest" and to act "in the name and in the person of Christ himself", and with his entire "life", called to manifest and witness in a fundamental way the "radicalism of the Gospel".[44]

CONFIGURATION TO CHRIST, THE HEAD AND SHEPHERD, AND PASTORAL CHARITY

21.   By sacramental consecration the priest is configured to Jesus Christ as Head and Shepherd of the Church, and he is endowed with a "spiritual power" which is a share in the authority with which Jesus Christ guides the Church through his Spirit.[45]

By virtue of this consecration brought about by the outpouring of the Spirit in the Sacrament of Holy Orders, the spiritual life of the priest is marked, moulded and characterized by the way of thinking and acting proper to Jesus Christ, Head and Shepherd of the Church, and which are summed up in his pastoral charity.

Jesus Christ is *Head of the Church, his Body.* He is the "Head" in the new and unique sense of being a "servant", according to his own words:

[44] Cf. *Propositio* 8.
[45] Cf. SECOND VATICAN ECUMENICAL COUNCIL, Decree on the Ministry and Life of Priests *Presbyterorum Ordinis,* 2; 12.

"The Son of man came not to be served but to serve, and to give his life as a ransom for many" (*Mk* 10:45). Jesus' service attains its fullest expression in his death on the Cross, that is, in his total gift of self in humility and love. "He emptied himself, taking the form of a servant, being born in the likeness of men. And being found in human form, he humbled himself and became obedient unto death, even death on a cross ..." (*Phil* 2:7-8). The authority of Jesus Christ as Head coincides then with his service, with his gift, with his total, humble and loving dedication on behalf of the Church. All this he did in perfect obedience to the Father; he is the one true suffering Servant of God, both Priest and Victim.

The spiritual existence of every priest receives its life and inspiration from exactly this type of authority, from service to the Church, precisely inasmuch as it is required by the priest's configuration to Jesus Christ Head and Servant of the Church.[46] As Saint Augustine once reminded a Bishop on the day of his ordination: "He who is head of the people must in the first place realize that he is to be the servant of many. And he should not disdain being such, I say it once again, he should not disdain being the servant of many, because the Lord of Lords did not disdain to make himself our servant".[47]

The spiritual life of the ministers of the New Testament should therefore be marked by this

---

[46] Cf. *Propositio* 8.
[47] *Sermo Morin Guelferbytanus*, 32, 1: *PLS* 2, 637.

fundamental attitude of service to the People of God (cf. *Mt* 20:24ff; *Mk* 10:43-44), freed from all presumption or desire of "lording over" those in their charge (cf. *1 Pt* 5:2-3). The priest is to perform this service freely and willingly as God desires. In this way the priests, as the ministers, the "elders" of the community, will be in their person the "model" of the flock, which, for its part, is called to display this same priestly attitude of service towards the world, in order to bring to humanity the fullness of life and complete liberation.

22.   The figure of Jesus Christ as *Shepherd of the Church, his flock,* takes up and re-presents in new and more evocative terms the same content as that of Jesus Christ as Head and Servant. Fulfilling the prophetic proclamation of the Messiah and Saviour joyfully announced by the psalmist and the Prophet Ezechiel (cf. *Ps* 22–23; *Ez* 34:11ff), Jesus presents himself as "the good Shepherd" (*Jn* 10:11, 14) not only of Israel but of all humanity (cf. *Jn* 10:16). His whole life is a continual manifestation of his "pastoral charity", or rather, a daily enactment of it. He feels compassion for the crowds because they were harassed and helpless, like sheep without a shepherd (cf. *Mt* 9:35-36). He goes in search of the straying and scattered sheep (cf. *Mt* 18:12-14) and joyfully celebrates their return. He gathers and protects them. He knows them and calls each one by name (cf. *Jn* 10:3). He leads them to green pastures and still waters (cf. *Ps* 22–23) and spreads a table for them, nourishing them with his own life. The

Good Shepherd offers this life through his own Death and Resurrection, as the Church sings out in the Roman Liturgy: "The Good Shepherd is risen! He who laid down his life for his sheep, who died for his flock, he is risen, alleluia".[48]

The author of the First Letter of Peter calls Jesus the "chief Shepherd" (*1 Pt* 5:4) because his work and mission continue in the Church through the Apostles (cf. *Jn* 21:15-17) and their successors (cf. *1 Pt* 5:1ff), and through priests. By virtue of their consecration, priests are configured to Jesus the Good Shepherd and are called to imitate and to live out his own pastoral charity.

Christ's gift of himself to his Church, the fruit of his love, is described in terms of that unique gift of self made by the Bridegroom to the Bride, as the sacred texts often suggest. *Jesus is the true Bridegroom* who offers to the Church the wine of salvation (cf. *Jn* 2:11). He who is "the Head of the Church, his body, and is himself its Saviour" (*Eph* 5:23) "loved the Church and gave himself up for her, that he might sanctify her, having cleansed her by the washing of water with the word, that he might present the Church to himself in splendour, without spot or wrinkle or any such thing, that she might be holy and without blemish" (*Eph* 5:25-27). The Church is indeed the body in which Christ the Head is present and active, but she is also the Bride who proceeds like a new Eve from the open side of the Redeemer on the Cross.

---

[48] ROMAN MISSAL, Communion Antiphon from the Mass of the Fourth Sunday of Easter.

Hence Christ stands "before" the Church, and "nourishes and cherishes her" (*Eph* 5:29), giving his life for her. The priest is called to be the living image of Jesus Christ, the Spouse of the Church.[49] Of course, he will always remain a member of the community as a believer alongside his other brothers and sisters who have been called by the Spirit, but in virtue of his configuration to Christ, the Head and Shepherd, the priest stands in this spousal relationship with regard to the community. "Inasmuch as he represents Christ, the Head, Shepherd and Spouse of the Church, the priest is placed not only in the Church but also in the forefront of the Church".[50] In his spiritual life, therefore, he is called to live out Christ's spousal love towards the Church, his Bride. Therefore, the priest's life ought to radiate this spousal character which demands that he be a witness to Christ's spousal love, and thus be capable of loving people with a heart which is new, generous and pure, with genuine self-detachment, with full, constant and faithful dedication and at the same time with a kind of "divine jealousy" (cf. *2 Cor* 11:2), and even with a kind of maternal tenderness, capable of bearing "the pangs of birth" until "Christ be formed" in the faithful (cf. *Gal* 4:19).

23. The internal principle, the force which animates and guides the spiritual life of the priest inasmuch as he is configured to Christ the Head

[49] Apostolic Letter *Mulieris Dignitatem* (15 August 1988), 26: *AAS* 80 (1988), 1715-1716.
[50] *Propositio* 7.

and Shepherd, is *pastoral charity,* as a participation in Jesus Christ's own pastoral charity, a gift freely bestowed by the Holy Spirit and likewise a task and a call which demand a free and committed response on the part of the priest.

The essential content of this pastoral charity is *the gift of self,* the total gift of *self to the Church,* following the example of Christ. "Pastoral charity is the virtue by which we imitate Christ in his self-giving and service. It is not just what we do, but our gift of self, which manifests Christ's love for his flock. Pastoral charity determines our way of thinking and acting, our way of relating to people. It makes special demands on us …".[51]

The gift of self, which is the source and synthesis of pastoral charity, is directed towards the Church. This was true of Christ who "loved the Church and gave himself up for her" (*Eph* 5:25) and the same must be true for the priest. With pastoral charity, which distinguishes the exercise of the priestly ministry as an *amoris officium,*[52] "the priest, who welcomes the call to ministry, is in a position to make this a loving choice, as a result of which the Church and souls become his first interest, and with this concrete spirituality he becomes capable of loving the universal Church and that part of it entrusted to him with the deep love of a husband for his wife".[53] The gift of self has no

[51] *Homily* at Eucharistic Adoration, Seoul (7 October 1989), 2: *Insegnamenti* XII/2 (1989), 785.

[52] SAINT AUGUSTINE, *In Iohannis Evangelium Tractatus* 123, 5: CCL 36, 678.

[53] *To priests* taking part in an assembly organized by the Italian Episcopal Conference (4 November 1980): *Insegnamenti* III/2 (1980), 1055.

58

limits, marked as it is by the same apostolic and missionary zeal of Christ, the Good Shepherd, who said: "And I have other sheep, that are not of this fold; I must bring them also, and they will heed my voice. So there shall be one flock, one shepherd" (*Jn* 10:16).

Within the Church community the priest's pastoral charity impels and demands in a particular and specific way his personal relationship with the presbyterate, united in and with the Bishop, as the Council explicitly states: "Pastoral charity requires that a priest always work in the bond of communion with the bishop and with his brother priests, lest his efforts be in vain".[54]

The gift of self to the Church concerns her insofar as she is the Body and the *Bride of Jesus Christ*. In this way the primary point of reference of the priest's charity is Jesus Christ himself. Only in loving and serving Christ the Head and Spouse will charity become a source, criterion, measure and impetus for the priest's love and service to the Church, the Body and Spouse of Christ. The Apostle Paul had a clear and sure understanding of this point. Writing to the Christians of the Church in Corinth, he refers to "ourselves as your servants for Jesus' sake" (*2 Cor* 4:5). Above all, this was the explicit and programmatic teaching of Jesus when he entrusted to Peter the ministry of shepherding the flock only after his threefold affirmation of love, indeed only after he had ex-

---

[54] Decree on the Ministry and Life of Priests *Presbyterorum Ordinis*, 14.

pressed a preferential love: "He said to him the third time, 'Simon, son of John, do you love me?' Peter ... said to him, 'Lord, you know everything; you know that I love you.' Jesus said to him, 'Feed my sheep...'" (*Jn* 21:17).

Pastoral charity, which has its specific source in the Sacrament of Holy Orders, finds its full expression and its supreme nourishment in the *Eucharist*. As the Council states: "This pastoral charity flows mainly from the Eucharistic Sacrifice, which is thus the centre and root of the whole priestly life. The priestly soul strives thereby to apply to itself the action which takes place on the altar of sacrifice".[55] Indeed, the Eucharist represents, makes once again present, the sacrifice of the Cross, the full gift of Christ to the Church, the gift of his Body given and his Blood shed, as the supreme witness of the fact that he is Head and Shepherd, Servant and Spouse of the Church. Precisely because of this, the priest's pastoral charity not only flows from the Eucharist but finds in the celebration of the Eucharist its highest realization, just as it is from the Eucharist that he receives the grace and obligation to give his whole life a "sacrificial" dimension.

This same pastoral charity is the dynamic inner principle capable of unifying the many different activities of the priest. In virtue of this pastoral charity the essential and permanent demand for unity between the priest's interior life and all his external actions and the obligations of the ministry

---

[55] *Ibid.*

can be properly fulfilled, a demand particularly urgent in a socio-cultural and ecclesial context strongly marked by complexity, fragmentation and dispersion. Only by directing every moment and every one of his acts towards the fundamental choice to "give his life for the flock" can the priest guarantee this unity which is vital and indispensable for his harmony and spiritual balance. The Council reminds us that "priests attain to the unity of their lives by uniting themselves with Christ whose food was to fulfil the will of him who sent him to do his work ... In this way, by assuming the role of the Good Shepherd they will find in the very exercise of pastoral charity the bond of priestly perfection which will unify their lives and activities".[56]

THE SPIRITUAL LIFE IN THE EXERCISE OF THE MINISTRY

24.   The Spirit of the Lord anointed Christ and sent him forth to announce the Gospel (cf. *Lk* 4:18). The priest's mission is not extraneous to his consecration or juxtaposed to it, but represents its intrinsic and vital purpose: *consecration is for mission.* In this sense, not only consecration but *mission as well is under the seal of the Spirit and the influence of his sanctifying power.*

This was the case in Jesus' life. This was the case in the lives of the Apostles and their successors. This is the case for the entire Church and

[56] *Ibid.*

within her for priests: all have received the Spirit as a gift and call to holiness in and through the carrying out of the mission.[57]

Therefore, an intimate bond exists between the priest's spiritual life and the exercise of his ministry,[58] a bond which the Council expresses in this fashion: "And so it is that they are grounded in the life of the Spirit while they exercise the ministry of the Spirit and of justice (cf. *2 Cor* 3:8-9), as long as they are docile to Christ's Spirit, who gives them life and guidance. For by their everyday sacred actions, as by the entire ministry which they exercise in union with the bishop and their fellow priests, they are being directed towards perfection of life. Priestly holiness itself contributes very greatly to a fruitful fulfilment of the priestly ministry".[59]

"Live the mystery that has been placed in your hands!" This is the invitation and admonition which the Church addresses to the priest in the Rite of Ordination, when the offerings of the holy people for the Eucharistic Sacrifice are placed in his hands. The "mystery" of which the priest is a "steward" (cf. *1 Cor* 4:1) is definitively Jesus Christ himself, who in the Spirit is the source of holiness and the call to sanctification. This "mystery" seeks expression in the priestly life. For this to be so, there is need for great vigilance and lively

[57] PAUL VI, Apostolic Exhortation *Evangelii Nuntiandi* (8 December 1975), 75: *AAS* 68 (1976), 64-67.

[58] Cf. *Propositio* 8.

[59] Decree on the Ministry and Life of Priests *Presbyterorum Ordinis*, 12.

awareness. Once again, the Rite of Ordination introduces these words with this recommendation: "be aware of what you will be doing". In the same way that Paul had admonished Timothy, "Do not neglect the gift you have" (*1 Tim* 4:14; cf. *2 Tim* 1:6).

The relation between a priest's spiritual life and the exercise of his ministry can also be explained on the basis of the pastoral charity bestowed by the Sacrament of Holy Orders. The ministry of the priest, precisely because of its participation in the saving ministry of Jesus Christ the Head and Shepherd, cannot fail to express and live out his pastoral charity which is both the source and spirit of his service and gift of self. In its objective reality the priestly ministry is an *"amoris officium"*, according to the previously-quoted expression of Saint Augustine. This objective reality itself serves as both the basis and requirement for a corresponding *ethos,* which can be none other than a life of love, as Saint Augustine himself points out: *Sit amoris officium pascere dominicum gregem.*[60] This *ethos* and as a result the spiritual life, is none other than embracing consciously and freely—that is to say in one's mind and heart, in one's decisions and actions—the "truth" of the priestly ministry as an *amoris officium.*

25.   For a spiritual life that grows through the exercise of the ministry, it is essential that the priest should continually renew and deepen his

---

[60] *In Iohannis Evangelium Tractatus* 123, 5: *loc. cit.*

awareness of being a minister of Jesus Christ by virtue of sacramental consecration and configuration to Christ the Head and Shepherd of the Church.

This awareness is not only in accordance with the very nature of the mission which the priest carries out on behalf of the Church and humanity, but it also provides a focus for the spiritual life of the priest who carries out that mission. Indeed, the priest is chosen by Christ not as an "object" but as a "person". In other words, he is not inert and passive, but rather is a "living instrument", as the Council states, precisely in the passage where it refers to the duty to pursue this perfection.[61] The Council also speaks of priests as "companions and helpers" of God who is "the holy one and sanctifier".[62]

In this way the exercise of his ministry deeply involves the priest himself as a conscious, free and responsible person. The bond with Jesus Christ assured by consecration and configuration to him in the Sacrament of Orders gives rise to and requires in the priest the further bond which comes from his "intention", that is, from a conscious and free choice to do in his ministerial activities what the Church intends to do. This bond tends by its very nature to become as extensive and profound as possible, affecting one's way of thinking, feeling and life itself: in other words, creating a series of moral and spiritual "dispositions" which corres-

---

[61] Cf. Decree on the Ministry and Life of Priests *Presbyterorum Ordinis*, 12.
[62] *Ibid.*, 5.

pond to the ministerial actions performed by the priest.

There can be no doubt that the exercise of the priestly ministry, especially in the celebration of the Sacraments, receives its saving effects from the action of Christ himself who becomes present in the Sacraments. But so as to emphasize the gratuitous nature of salvation which makes a person both "saved" and a "saviour"—always and only in Christ—God's plan has ordained that the efficacy of the exercise of the ministry is also conditioned by a greater or lesser human receptivity and participation.[63] In particular, the greater or lesser degree of the holiness of the minister has a real effect on the proclamation of the word, the celebration of the Sacraments and the leadership of the community in charity. This was clearly stated by the Council: "The very holiness of priests is of the greatest benefit for the fruitful fulfilment of their ministry. While it is possible for God's grace to carry out the work of salvation through unworthy ministers, yet God ordinarily prefers to show his wonders through those men who are more submissive to the impulse and guidance of the Holy Spirit and who, because of their intimate union with Christ and their holiness of life, are able to say with Saint Paul: 'It is no longer I who live, but Christ who lives in me' (*Gal* 2:20)".[64]

The consciousness that one is a minister of

[63] Cf. COUNCIL OF TRENT, Decree on Justification, cap. 7; Decree on Sacraments, can. 6.
[64] Decree on the Ministry and Life of Priests *Presbyterorum Ordinis,* 12.

Jesus Christ the Head and Shepherd also brings with it a thankful and joyful awareness that one has received a singular grace and treasure from Jesus Christ: the grace of having been freely chosen by the Lord to be a "living instrument" in the work of salvation. This choice bears witness to Jesus Christ's love for the priest. This love, like other loves and yet even more so, demands a response. After his Resurrection, Jesus asked Peter the basic question about love: "Simon, son of John, do you love me more than these?". And following his response Jesus entrusts Peter with the mission: "Feed my lambs" (*Jn* 21:15). Jesus first asks Peter if he loves him so as to be able to entrust his flock to him. However, in reality it was Christ's own love, free and unsolicited, which gave rise to his question to Peter and to his act of entrusting "his" sheep to Peter. Therefore, every ministerial action, while it leads to loving and serving the Church, provides an incentive to grow in ever greater love and service of Jesus Christ the Head, Shepherd and Spouse of the Church, a love which is always a response to the free and unsolicited love of God in Christ. Growth in the love of Jesus Christ determines in turn the growth of love for the Church: "We are your shepherds (*pascimus vobis*), with you we receive nourishment (*pascimur vobiscum*). May the Lord give us the strength to love you to the extent of dying for you, either in fact or in desire (*aut effectu aut affectu*)".[65]

[65] SAINT AUGUSTINE, *Sermo de Nat. Sanct. Apost. Petri et Pauli ex Evangelio in quo ait: Simon Iohannis diligis me?*: *Bibliotheca Casi-*

26.   Thanks to the insightful teaching of the
Second Vatican Council,[66] we can grasp the conditions and demands, the manifestations and fruits
of the intimate bond between the priest's spiritual
life and the exercise of his threefold ministry of
word, sacrament and pastoral charity.

The priest is first of all a *minister of the Word
of God*. He is consecrated and sent forth to proclaim the Good News of the Kingdom to all, calling every person to the obedience of faith and
leading believers to an ever-increasing knowledge
of and communion in the mystery of God, as revealed and communicated to us in Christ. For this
reason, the priest himself ought first of all to develop a great personal familiarity with the word
of God. Knowledge of its linguistic or exegetical
aspects, though certainly necessary, is not enough.
He needs to approach the word with a docile and
prayerful heart, so that it may deeply penetrate
his thoughts and feelings and bring about a new
outlook in him—"the mind of Christ" (*1 Cor*
2:16)—such that his words and his choices and
attitudes may become ever more a reflection, a
proclamation and a witness to the Gospel. Only if
he "abides" in the word will the priest become a
perfect disciple of the Lord. Only then will he
know the truth and be set truly free, overcoming
every conditioning which is contrary or foreign to
the Gospel (cf. *Jn* 8:31-32). The priest ought to be

---

nensis, in "Miscellenea Augustiniana", vol. 1, ed. G. Morin,
O.S.B., Rome, Typ. Poligl. Vat., 1930, p. 404.
    [66] Cf. Decree on the Ministry and Life of Priests *Presbyterorum
Ordinis,* 4-6; 13.

the first "believer" in the word, while being fully aware that the words of his ministry are not "his", but those of the One who sent him. He is not the master of the word, but its servant. He is not the sole possessor of the word; in its regard he is in debt to the People of God. Precisely because he can and does evangelize, the priest, like every other member of the Church, ought to grow in awareness that he himself is continually in need of being evangelized.[67] He proclaims the word in his capacity as "minister", as a sharer in the prophetic authority of Christ and the Church. As a result, in order that he himself may possess and give to the faithful the guarantee that he is transmitting the Gospel in its fullness, the priest is called to develop a special sensitivity, love and docility to the living Tradition of the Church and to her Magisterium. These are not foreign to the word, but serve its proper interpretation and preserve its authentic meaning.[68]

It is above all in the *celebration of the Sacraments* and in the celebration of the Liturgy of the Hours that the priest is called to live and witness to the deep unity between the exercise of his ministry and his spiritual life. The gift of grace offered to the Church becomes the principle of holiness and a call to sanctification. For the priest as well, the truly central place, both in his ministry and spiritual life, belongs to the Eucharist, since in

[67] Cf. PAUL VI, Apostolic Exhortation *Evangelii Nuntiandi* (8 December 1975), 15: *loc. cit.,* 13-15.
[68] Cf. Dogmatic Constitution on Divine Revelation *Dei Verbum,* 8, 10.

it is contained "the whole spiritual good of the Church, namely Christ himself our Pasch and the living bread which gives life to men through his flesh—that flesh which is given life and gives life through the Holy Spirit. Thus people are invited and led to offer themselves, their works and all creation with Christ".[69]

From the various Sacraments, and in particular from the specific grace proper to each of them, the priest's spiritual life receives certain features. It is built up and moulded by the different characteristics and demands of each of the Sacraments as he celebrates them and experiences them.

I would like to make special mention of the Sacrament of Penance, of which priests are the ministers, but ought also to be its beneficiaries, becoming themselves witnesses of God's mercy towards sinners. Once again, I would like to set forth what I wrote in the Exhortation *Reconciliatio et Paenitentia:* "The priest's spiritual and pastoral life, like that of his brothers and sisters, lay and religious, depends, for its quality and fervour, on the frequent and conscientious personal practice of the Sacrament of Penance. The priest's celebration of the Eucharist and administration of the other Sacraments, his pastoral zeal, his relationship with the faithful, his communion with his brother priests, his collaboration with his Bishop, his life of prayer—in a word, the whole of his priestly existence, suffers an inexorable decline if

---

[69] SECOND VATICAN ECUMENICAL COUNCIL, Decree on the Ministry and Life of Priests *Presbyterorum Ordinis,* 5.

by negligence or for some other reason he fails to receive the Sacrament of Penance at regular intervals and in a spirit of genuine faith and devotion. If a priest were no longer to go to confession or properly confess his sins, his *priestly being* and his *priestly action* would feel its effects very soon, and this would also be noticed by the community of which he was the pastor".[70]

Finally, the priest is called to express in his life the authority and service of Jesus Christ the Head and Priest of the Church by *encouraging and leading the ecclesial community,* that is, by gathering together "the family of God as a fellowship endowed with the spirit of unity" and by leading it "in Christ through the Spirit to God the Father".[71] This *munus regendi* represents a very delicate and complex duty which, in addition to the attention which must be given to a variety of persons and their vocations, also involves the ability to coordinate all the gifts and charisms which the Spirit inspires in the community, to discern them and to put them to good use for the upbuilding of the Church in constant union with the Bishops. This ministry demands of the priest an intense spiritual life, filled with those qualities and virtues which are typical of a person who "presides over" and "leads" a community, of an "elder" in the noblest and richest sense of the word: qualities and virtues such as faithfulness, integrity, consistency,

---

[70] Post-Synodal Apostolic Exhortation *Reconciliatio et Paenitentia* (2 December 1984), 31, VI: *AAS* 77 (1985), 265-266.
[71] SECOND VATICAN ECUMENICAL COUNCIL, Decree on the Ministry and Life of Priests *Presbyterorum Ordinis,* 6.

wisdom, a welcoming spirit, friendliness, goodness
of heart, decisive firmness in essentials, freedom
from overly subjective viewpoints, personal disin-
terestedness, patience, an enthusiasm for daily
tasks, confidence in the value of the hidden work-
ings of grace as manifested in the simple and the
poor (cf. *Tit* 1:7-8).

PRIESTLY LIFE AND THE RADICALISM OF THE GOSPEL

27.   "The Spirit of the Lord is upon me" (*Lk*
4:18). The Holy Spirit poured out in the Sacrament of Holy Orders is a source of holiness and a
call to sanctification. This is the case not only because it configures the priest to Christ, the Head
and Shepherd of the Church, entrusting him with
a prophetic, priestly and royal mission to be carried out in the name and person of Christ, but
also because it inspires and enlivens his daily existence, enriching it with gifts and demands, virtues
and incentives which are summed up in pastoral
charity. This charity is a synthesis which unifies
the values and virtues contained in the Gospel and
likewise a power which sustains their development
towards Christian perfection.[72]

For all Christians without exception, the radicalism of the Gospel represents a fundamental,
undeniable demand flowing from the call of Christ
to follow and imitate him by virtue of the intimate

[72] Cf. SECOND VATICAN ECUMENICAL COUNCIL, Dogmatic
Constitution on the Church *Lumen Gentium*, 42.

71

communion of life with him brought about by the Spirit (cf. *Mt* 8:18ff; 10:37ff; *Mk* 8:34-38; 10:17-21; *Lk* 9:57ff). This same demand is made anew to priests, not only because they are "in" the Church, but because they are "in the forefront" of the Church, inasmuch as they are configured to Christ, the Head and Shepherd, equipped for and committed to the ordained ministry, and inspired by pastoral charity. Within and as a manifestation of the radicalism of the Gospel one can find a blossoming of many virtues and ethical demands which are decisive for the pastoral and spiritual life of the priest, such as faith, humility in relation to the mystery of God, mercy and prudence. A particularly significant expression of the radicalism of the Gospel is seen in the different "evangelical counsels" which Jesus proposes in the Sermon on the Mount (cf. *Mt* 5-7), and among them the intimately related counsels of obedience, chastity and poverty.[73] The priest is called to live these counsels in accordance with those ways and, more specifically, those goals and that basic meaning which derive from and express his own priestly identity.

28.   "Among the virtues most necessary for the priestly ministry must be named that disposition of soul by which priests are always ready to seek not their own will, but the will of him who sent them (cf. *Jn* 4:34; 5:30; 6:38)".[74] It is in the

[73] Cf. *Propositio* 9.
[74] SECOND VATICAN ECUMENICAL COUNCIL, Decree on the Ministry and Life of Priests *Presbyterorum Ordinis*, 15.

spiritual life of the priest that obedience takes on certain special characteristics.

First of all, obedience is *"apostolic"* in the sense that it recognizes, loves and serves the Church in her hierarchical structure. Indeed, there can be no genuine priestly ministry except in communion with the Supreme Pontiff and the Episcopal College, especially with one's own diocesan Bishop, who deserves that "filial respect and obedience" promised during the rite of ordination. This "submission" to those invested with ecclesial authority is in no way a kind of humiliation. It flows instead from the responsible freedom of the priest who accepts not only the demands of an organized and organic ecclesial life, but also that grace of discernment and responsibility in ecclesial decisions which was assured by Jesus to his Apostles and their successors, for the sake of faithfully safeguarding the mystery of the Church and serving the structure of the Christian community along its common path towards salvation.

Authentic Christian obedience, when it is properly motivated and lived without servility, helps the priest to exercise in accordance with the Gospel the authority entrusted to him for his work with the People of God: an authority free from authoritarianism or demagogery. Only the person who knows how to obey in Christ is really able to require obedience from others in accordance with the Gospel.

Priestly obedience has also a *"community" dimension:* it is not the obedience of an individual who alone relates to authority, but rather an obedience which is deeply a part of the unity of the presbyterate, which as such is called to cooperate harmoniously with the Bishop and, through him, with Peter's successor.[75]

This aspect of the priest's obedience demands a marked spirit of asceticism, both in the sense of a tendency not to become too bound up in one's own preferences or points of view, and in the sense of giving brother priests the opportunity to make good use of their talents and abilities, setting aside all forms of jealousy, envy and rivalry. Priestly obedience should be one of solidarity, based on belonging to a single presbyterate. Within the presbyterate, this obedience is expressed in co-responsibility regarding directions to be taken and choices to be made.

Finally, priestly obedience has a particular *"pastoral" character*. It is lived in an atmosphere of constant readiness to allow oneself to be taken up, as it were "consumed", by the needs and demands of the flock. These last ought to be truly reasonable and at times they need to be evaluated and tested to see how genuine they are. But it is undeniable that the priest's life is fully "taken up" by the hunger for the Gospel and for faith, hope and love for God and his mystery, a hunger which is more or less consciously present in the People of God entrusted to him.

29.   Referring to the evangelical counsels, the Council states that "preeminent among these

[75] Cf. *ibid*.

counsels is that precious gift of divine grace given to some by the Father (cf. *Mt* 19:11; *1 Cor* 7:7) in order more easily to devote themselves to God alone with an undivided heart (cf. *1 Cor* 7:32-34) in virginity or celibacy. This perfect continence for love of the Kingdom of Heaven has always been held in high esteem by the Church as a sign and stimulus of love, and as a singular source of spiritual fertility in the world".[76] In virginity and celibacy, chastity retains its original meaning, that is, of human sexuality lived as a genuine sign of and precious service to the love of communion and gift of self to others. This meaning is fully found in virginity which makes evident, even in the renunciation of marriage, the "nuptial meaning" of the body through a communion and a personal gift to Jesus Christ and his Church which prefigures and anticipates the perfect and final communion and self-giving of the world to come: "In virginity or celibacy, the human being is awaiting, also in a bodily way, the eschatological marriage of Christ with the Church, giving himself or herself completely to the Church in the hope that Christ may give himself to the Church in the full truth of eternal life".[77]

In this light one can more easily understand and appreciate the reasons behind the centuries-old choice which the Western Church has made and maintained—despite all the difficulties and objections raised down the centuries—of

[76] Dogmatic Constitution on the Church *Lumen Gentium*, 42.
[77] Apostolic Exhortation *Familiaris Consortio* (22 November 1981), 16: *AAS* 74 (1982), 98.

conferring the Order of Presbyter only on men who have given proof that they have been called by God to the gift of chastity in absolute and perpetual celibacy.

The Synod Fathers clearly and forcefully expressed their thought on this matter in an important proposal which deserves to be quoted here in full: "While in no way interfering with the discipline of the Oriental Churches, the Synod, in the conviction that perfect chastity in priestly celibacy is a charism, reminds priests that celibacy is a priceless gift of God for the Church and has a prophetic value for the world today. This Synod strongly reaffirms what the Latin Church and some Oriental Rites require, that is, that the priesthood be conferred only on those men who have received from God the gift of the vocation to celibate chastity (without prejudice to the tradition of some Oriental Churches and particular cases of married clergy who convert to Catholicism, which are admitted as exceptions in Pope Paul VI's Encyclical on priestly celibacy, No. 42). The Synod does not wish to leave any doubts in the mind of anyone regarding the Church's firm will to maintain the law that demands perpetual and freely chosen celibacy for present and future candidates for priestly ordination in the Latin Rite. The Synod would like to see celibacy presented and explained in the fullness of its biblical, theological and spiritual richness, as a precious gift given by God to his Church and as a sign of the Kingdom which is not of this world, a sign of God's love for this world and of the undivided love of the priest for God and for God's People, with the result that celibacy is seen as a positive enrichment of the priesthood".[78]

It is especially important that the priest understand the theological motivation of the Church's law on celibacy. Inasmuch as it is a law, it expresses *the Church's will,* even before the will of the subject expressed by his readiness. But the will of the Church finds its ultimate motivation in the *link between celibacy and sacred Ordination,* which configures the priest to Jesus Christ the Head and Spouse of the Church. The Church, as the Spouse of Jesus Christ, wishes to be loved by the priest in the total and exclusive manner in which Jesus Christ her Head and Spouse loved her. Priestly celibacy, then, is the gift of self *in* and *with* Christ *to* his Church and expresses the priest's service to the Church in and with the Lord.

For an adequate priestly spiritual life, celibacy ought not to be considered and lived as an isolated or purely negative element, but as one aspect of a positive, specific and characteristic approach to being a priest. Leaving father and mother, the priest follows Jesus the Good Shepherd, in an apostolic communion, in the service of the People of God. Celibacy, then, is to be welcomed and continually renewed with a free and loving decision as a priceless gift from God, as an "incentive to pastoral charity",[79] as a singular sharing in God's fatherhood and in the fruitfulness of the Church,

---

[78] *Propositio* 11.
[79] SECOND VATICAN ECUMENICAL COUNCIL, Decree on the Ministry and Life of Priests *Presbyterorum Ordinis,* 16.

and as a witness to the world of the eschatological Kingdom. To put into practice all the moral, pastoral and spiritual demands of priestly celibacy it is absolutely necessary that the priest pray humbly and trustingly, as the Council points out: "In the world today, many people call perfect continence impossible. The more they do so, the more humbly and perseveringly priests should join with the Church in praying for the grace of fidelity. It is never denied to those who ask. At the same time let priests make use of all the supernatural and natural helps which are now available to all".[80] Once again it is prayer, together with the Church's Sacraments and ascetical practice, which will provide hope in difficulties, forgiveness in failings, and confidence and courage in resuming the journey.

30.   On the subject of *evangelical poverty,* the Synod Fathers gave a concise yet important description, presenting it as "the subjection of all goods to the supreme good of God and his Kingdom".[81] In reality, only the person who contemplates and lives the mystery of God as the one and supreme good, as the true and definitive treasure, can understand and practise poverty, which is certainly not a matter of despising or rejecting material goods, but of a loving and responsible use of these goods and at the same time an ability to renounce them with great interior freedom, that is, with reference to God and his plan.

[80] *Ibid.*
[81] *Propositio* 8.

Poverty for the priest, by virtue of his sacramental configuration to Christ, the Head and Shepherd, takes on specific "pastoral" connotations which the Synod Fathers took up from the Council's teaching [82] and further developed. Among other things, they wrote: "Priests, following the example of Christ who rich though he was became poor for love of us (cf. *2 Cor* 8:9), should consider the poor and the weakest as people entrusted in a special way to them and they should be capable of witnessing to poverty with a simple and austere lifestyle, having learned the generous renunciation of superfluous things (*Optatam Totius,* 9; *C.I.C.,* can. 282)".[83]

It is true that "the workman deserves his wages" (*Lk* 10:7) and that "the Lord commanded that those who proclaim the Gospel should get their living by the Gospel" (*1 Cor* 9:14), but it is no less true that this right of the Apostle can in no way be confused with attempts of any kind to condition service to the Gospel and the Church upon the advantages and interests which can derive from it. Poverty alone ensures that the priest remains available to be sent wherever his work will be most useful and needed, even at the cost of personal sacrifice. It is a condition and essential premise of the Apostle's docility to the Spirit, making him ready to "go forth", without travelling bag or personal ties, following only the will of the Master (cf. *Lk* 9:57-62; *Mk* 10:17-22).

---

[82] Cf. Decree on the Ministry and Life of Priests *Presbyterorum Ordinis,* 17.
[83] *Propositio* 10.

79

Being personally involved in the life of the community and being responsible for it, the priest should also offer the witness of a total "honesty" in the administration of the goods of the community, which he will never treat as if they were his own property, but rather something for which he will be held accountable by God and his brothers and sisters, especially the poor. Moreover, his awareness of belonging to the one presbyterate will be an incentive for the priest to commit himself to promoting both a more equitable distribution of goods among his fellow priests and a certain common use of goods (cf. *Acts* 2:42-47).

The interior freedom which is safeguarded and nourished by evangelical poverty will help the priest to stand beside the underprivileged, to practise solidarity with their efforts to create a more just society, to be more sensitive and capable of understanding and discerning realities involving the economic and social aspects of life, and to promote a preferential option for the poor. The latter, while excluding no one from the proclamation and gift of salvation, will assist him in gently approaching the poor, sinners, and all those on the margins of society, following the model given by Jesus in carrying out his prophetic and priestly ministry (cf. *Lk* 4:18).

Nor should the prophetic significance of priestly poverty be forgotten, so urgently needed in affluent and consumeristic societies: "A truly poor priest is indeed a specific sign of separation from, disavowal of and non-submission to the tyranny of a contemporary world which puts all its trust in money and in material security".[84]

Jesus Christ, who brought his pastoral charity to perfection on the Cross with a complete exterior and interior emptying of self, is both the model and source of the virtues of obedience, chastity and poverty which the priest is called to live out as an expression of his pastoral charity for his brothers and sisters. In accordance with Saint Paul's words to the Christians at Philippi, the priest should have "the mind which was in Christ Jesus", emptying himself of his own "self", so as to discover, in a charity which is obedient, chaste and poor, the royal road of union with God and unity with his brothers and sisters (cf. *Phil* 2:5).

MEMBERSHIP IN AND DEDICATION TO THE PARTICULAR CHURCH

31.   Like every authentically Christian spiritual life, the spiritual life of the priest has an *essential and undeniable ecclesial dimension* which is a sharing in the holiness of the Church herself, which we profess in the *Creed* to be a "Communion of Saints". The holiness of the Christian has its source in the holiness of the Church; it expresses that holiness and at the same time enriches it. This ecclesial dimension takes on special forms, purposes and meanings in the spiritual life of the

[84] *Ibid.*

priest by virtue of his specific relation to the Church, always as a result of his configuration to Christ the Head and Shepherd, his ordained ministry and his pastoral charity.

In this perspective, it is necessary to consider the priest's membership in and dedication to a particular Church. These two factors are not the result of purely organizational and disciplinary needs. On the contrary, the priest's relationship with his Bishop in the one presbyterate, his sharing in the Bishop's ecclesial concern, and his devotion to the evangelical care of the People of God in the specific historical and contextual conditions of a particular Church are elements which must be taken into account in sketching the proper configuration of the priest and his spiritual life. In this sense, "incardination" cannot be confined to a purely juridical bond, but also involves a set of attitudes as well as spiritual and pastoral decisions which help to fill out the specific features of the priestly vocation.

The priest needs to be aware that his "being in a particular Church" constitutes by its very nature a significant element in his living a Christian spirituality. In this sense, the priest finds precisely in his belonging to and dedication to the particular Church a wealth of meaning, criteria for discernment and action which shape both his pastoral mission and his spiritual life.

Other insights or reference to other traditions of spiritual life can contribute to the priest's journey towards perfection, for these are capable of enriching the life of individual priests as well as enlivening the presbyterate with precious spiritual gifts. Such is the case with many old and new Church associations which welcome priests into their spiritual family: from societies of apostolic life to priestly secular institutes, and from various forms of spiritual communion and sharing to ecclesial Movements. Priests who belong to religious orders and congregations represent a spiritual enrichment for the entire diocesan presbyterate, to which they contribute specific charisms and special ministries, stimulating the particular Church by their presence to be more intensely open to the Church throughout the world.[85]

The priest's membership in a particular Church and his dedication—even to the gift of his life—to the upbuilding of the Church, "in the person" of Christ the Head and Shepherd, in service of the entire Christian community and in a generous and filial relationship with the Bishop, must be strengthened by every charism which becomes part of his priestly life or surrounds it.[86]

For the abundance of the Spirit's gifts to be welcomed with joy and allowed to bear fruit for the glory of God and the good of the entire Church, each person is required first to have a knowledge and discernment of his or her own charisms and those of others, and always to use these charisms with Christian humility, with firm

[85] Cf. SACRED CONGREGATION FOR RELIGIOUS AND SECULAR INSTITUTES and SACRED CONGREGATION FOR BISHOPS, Directives for Mutual Relations between Bishops and Religious in the Church Mutuae Relationes, (14 May 1978), 18: AAS 70 1978, 484-485.

[86] Cf. Propositio 25; 38.

self-control and with the intention, above all else, to help build up the entire community which each particular charism is meant to serve. Moreover, all are required to make a sincere effort to live in mutual esteem, to respect others and to hold in esteem all the positive and legitimate diversities present in the presbyterate. This too constitutes part of the priest's spiritual life and his continual practice of asceticism.

32.   Membership in and dedication to a particular Church does not limit the activity and life of the presbyterate to that Church: a restriction of this sort is not possible, given the very nature both of the particular Church [87] and of the priestly ministry. In this regard the Council teaches that "the spiritual gift which priests received at their ordination prepares them not for any limited or narrow mission but for the widest scope of the universal mission of salvation 'to the end of the earth' (*Acts* 1:8). For every priestly ministry shares in the universality of the mission entrusted by Christ to his Apostles". [88]

It thus follows that the spiritual life of the priest should be profoundly marked by a missionary zeal and dynamism. In the exercise of their ministry and the witness of their lives, priests have the duty to form the community entrusted to them as a truly missionary community. As I wrote

[87] Cf. SECOND VATICAN ECUMENICAL COUNCIL, Dogmatic Constitution on the Church *Lumen Gentium*, 23.
[88] Decree on Ministry and Life of Priests *Presbyterorum Ordinis*, 10; cf. *Propositio* 12.

in the Encyclical *Redemptoris Missio,* "all priests must have the mind and heart of missionaries open to the needs of the Church and the world, with concern for those farthest away, and especially for the non-Christian groups in their own area. They should have at heart, in their prayers and particularly at the Eucharistic Sacrifice, the concern of the whole Church for all of humanity".[89]

If the lives of priests are generously inspired by this missionary spirit, it will be easier to respond to that increasingly serious demand of the Church today which arises from the unequal distribution of the clergy. In this regard, the Council was both quite clear and forceful: "Let priests remember then that they must have at heart the care of all the Churches. Hence priests belonging to dioceses which are rich in vocations should show themselves willing and ready, with the permission or at the urging of their own Bishop, to exercise their ministry in other regions, missions, or activities which suffer from a shortage of clergy".[90]

"RENEW IN THEM THE OUTPOURING OF YOUR SPIRIT OF HOLINESS"

33.   "The Spirit of the Lord is upon me, because he has anointed me to preach good news to the poor..." (*Lk* 4:18). Even today Christ

---

[89] Encyclical Letter *Redemptoris Missio* (7 December 1990), 67: *AAS* 83 (1991), 315-316.
[90] Decree on the Ministry and Life of Priests *Presbyterorum Ordinis,* 10.

makes these words which he proclaimed in the synagogue of Nazareth echo in our priestly hearts. Indeed, our faith reveals to us the presence of the Spirit of Christ at work in our being, in our acting, and in our living, just as the Sacrament of Orders has configured, equipped and moulded it.

Yes, the Spirit of the Lord is the principal agent in our spiritual life. He creates our "new heart", inspires it and guides it with the "new law" of love, of pastoral charity. For the development of the spiritual life it is essential to be aware that the priest will never lack the grace of the Holy Spirit, as a totally gratuitous gift and as a task which he is called to undertake. Awareness of this gift is the foundation and support of the priest's unflagging trust amid the difficulties, temptations and weaknesses which he will meet along his spiritual path.

Here I would repeat to all priests what I said to so many of them on another occasion: "The priestly vocation is essentially a call to holiness, in the form which derives from the Sacrament of Orders. Holiness is intimacy with God; it is the imitation of Christ, who was poor, chaste and humble; it is unreserved love for souls and a giving of oneself on their behalf and for their true good; it is love for the Church which is holy and wants us to be holy, because this is the mission that Christ entrusted to her. Each one of you should also be holy in order to help your brothers and sisters to pursue their vocation to holiness.

"How can we fail to reflect on... the essential role that the Holy Spirit carries out in this particular call to holiness which is proper to the priestly ministry? Let us remember the words of the rite of priestly ordination which are considered to be central in the sacramental formula: 'Almighty Father, give these your sons, the dignity of the priesthood. Renew in them the outpouring of your Spirit of holiness. O Lord, may they fulfil the ministry of the second degree of priesthood received from you and by their example may they lead all to upright conduct of life'.

"Beloved, through Ordination, you have received the same Spirit of Christ, who makes you like him, so that you can act in his name and so that his very mind and heart might live in you. This intimate communion with the Spirit of Christ, while guaranteeing the efficacy of the sacramental actions which you perform *in persona Christi,* seeks to be expressed in fervent prayer, in integrity of life, in the pastoral charity of a ministry tirelessly spending itself for the salvation of the brethren. In a word, it calls for your personal sanctification".[91]

---

[91] *Homily* to 5,000 priests from throughout the world (9 October 1984), 2: *Insegnamenti* VII/2 (1984), 839.

CHAPTER IV

COME AND SEE

PRIESTLY VOCATION
IN THE CHURCH'S PASTORAL WORK

SEEK, FOLLOW, ABIDE

34. *"Come, and see"* (*Jn* 1:39). This was
the reply Jesus gave to the two disciples of
John the Baptist who asked him where he was
staying. In these words we find the meaning of
vocation.

This is how the Evangelist relates the call of
Andrew and Peter: "The next day again John was
standing with two of his disciples; and he looked
at Jesus as he walked, and said, 'Behold, the
Lamb of God!' The two disciples heard him
say this, and they followed Jesus. Jesus turned,
and saw them following, and said to them, 'What
do you seek?' And they said to him, 'Rabbi'
(which means Teacher), 'where are you staying?'
He said to them, 'Come and see.' They came
and saw where he was staying; and they stayed
with him that day, for it was about the tenth
hour.

"One of the two who heard John speak, and
followed him, was Andrew, Simon Peter's

88

brother. He first found his brother Simon, and said to him, 'We have found the Messiah' (which means Christ). He brought him to Jesus. Jesus looked at him, and said, 'So you are Simon the son of John? You shall be called Cephas' (which means Peter)" (*Jn* 1:35-42).

This Gospel passage is one of many in the Bible where the "mystery" of vocation is described, in our case the mystery of the vocation to be Apostles of Jesus. This passage of John, which is also significant for the Christian vocation as such, has a particular value with regard to the priestly vocation. As the community of Jesus' disciples, the Church is called to contemplate this scene which in some way is renewed constantly down the ages. The Church is invited to delve more deeply into the original and personal meaning of the call to follow Christ in the priestly ministry and the unbreakable bond between divine grace and human responsibility which is contained and revealed in these two terms which we find more than once in the Gospel: *come, follow me* (cf. *Mt* 19:21). She is asked to discern and to live out the proper dynamism of vocation, its gradual and concrete development in the phases of *seeking Christ, finding him* and *staying with him.*

The Church gathers from this *"Gospel of vocation"* the paradigm, strength and impulse behind her pastoral work of promoting vocations, of her mission to care for the birth, discernment and fostering of vocations, particularly those to the priesthood. By the very fact that "the lack of priests is certainly a sad thing for any Church",[92] pastoral work for vocations needs, especially today, to be taken up with a new vigour and more decisive commitment by all the members of the Church, in the awareness that it is not a secondary or marginal matter, or the business of one group only, as if it were but a "part", no matter how important, of the entire pastoral work of the Church. Rather, as the Synod Fathers frequently repeated, it is an essential part of the overall pastoral work of each Church,[93] a concern which demands to be integrated into and fully identified with the ordinary "care of souls",[94] a connatural and essential dimension of the Church's pastoral work, of her very life and mission.[95]

Indeed, *concern for vocations is a connatural and essential dimension of the Church's pastoral work.* The reason for this is that vocation, in a certain sense, defines the very being of the Church, even before her activity. In the Church's very name, *Ecclesia,* we find its deep vocational aspect, for the Church is a "convocation", an *assembly of those who have been called:* "All those, who in faith look towards Jesus, the author of salvation and the principle of unity and peace, God has gathered together and established as the Church, that

---

[92] *Discourse at the end of the Synod* (27 October 1990), 5: *loc. cit.*
[93] Cf. *Propositio* 6.
[94] Cf. *Propositio* 13.
[95] Cf. *Propositio* 4.

she may be for each and everyone the visible sacrament of this saving unity".[96]

A genuinely theological assessment of priestly vocation and pastoral work in its regard can only arise from an assessment of the mystery of the Church as a *mysterium vocationis.*

THE CHURCH AND THE GIFT OF VOCATION

35.   Every Christian vocation finds its foundation in the gratuitous and prevenient choice made by the Father "who has blessed us in Christ with every spiritual blessing in the heavenly places, even as he chose us in him before the foundation of the world, that we should be holy and blameless before him. He destined us in love to be his sons through Jesus Christ, according to the purpose of his will" (*Eph* 1:3-5).

Each Christian vocation comes from God and is God's gift. However, it is never bestowed outside of or independently of the Church. Instead it always comes about in the Church and through the Church because, as the Second Vatican Council reminds us, "God has willed to make men holy and save them, not as individuals without any bond or link between them, but rather to make them into a people who might acknowledge him and serve him in holiness".[97]

The Church not only embraces in herself all the vocations which God gives her along the path

[96] SECOND VATICAN ECUMENICAL COUNCIL Dogmatic Constitution on the Church *Lumen Gentium*, 9.
[97] *Ibid.*

to salvation, but she herself appears as a mystery of vocation, a luminous and living reflection of the mystery of the Blessed Trinity. In truth, the Church, a "people made one by the unity of the Father, the Son and the Holy Spirit",[98] carries within her the mystery of the Father, who, being neither called nor sent by any one (cf. *Rom* 11:33-35), calls all to hallow his name and do his will; she guards within herself the mystery of the Son, who is called by the Father and sent to proclaim the Kingdom of God to all and who calls all to follow him; and she is the trustee of the mystery of the Holy Spirit, who consecrates for mission those whom the Father calls through his Son Jesus Christ.

The Church, being by her very nature a "vocation", is also a *begetter and educator of vocations.* This is so because she is a "sacrament", a "sign" and "instrument" in which the vocation of every Christian is reflected and lived out. And she is so in her activity, in the exercise of her ministry of proclaiming the Word, in her celebration of the Sacraments and in her service and witness to charity.

We can now see the *essential dimension of the Christian vocation:* not only does it derive "from" the Church and her mediation, not only does it come to be known and find fulfilment "in" the Church, but it also necessarily appears—in fundamental service to God—as a service "to" the Church. Christian vocation, whatever shape it

[98] SAINT CYPRIAN, *De Dominica Oratione*, 23: *CCL* 3/A, 105.

takes, is a gift whose purpose is to build up the Church and to increase the Kingdom of God in the world.[99]

What is true of every vocation, is true specifically of the priestly vocation: the latter is a call, by the Sacrament of Holy Orders received in the Church, to place oneself at the service of the People of God with a particular belonging and configuration to Jesus Christ and with the authority of acting "in the name and in the person" of him who is Head and Shepherd of the Church.

From this point of view, we understand the statement of the Synod Fathers: "The vocation of each priest exists in the Church and for the Church: through her this vocation is brought to fulfilment. Hence we can say that every priest receives his vocation from our Lord through the Church as a gracious gift, a grace *gratis data (charisma)*. It is the task of the Bishop or the competent superior not only to examine the suitability and the vocation of the candidate but also to recognize it. This ecclesiastical element is inherent in a vocation to the priestly ministry as such. The candidate to the priesthood should receive his vocation not by imposing his own personal conditions, but accepting also the norms and conditions which the Church herself lays down, in the fulfilment of her responsibility".[100]

[99] Cf. SECOND VATICAN ECUMENICAL COUNCIL, Decree on the Apostolate of the Laity *Apostolicam Actuositatem*, 3.
[100] *Propositio* 5.

The vocational dialogue: divine initiative and human response

36.   The history of every priestly vocation, as indeed of every Christian vocation, is the history of an *inexpressible dialogue between God and human beings,* between the love of God who calls and the freedom of individuals who respond lovingly to him. These two indivisible aspects of vocation, God's gratuitous gift and man's responsible freedom, are reflected in a splendid and very effective way in the brief words with which the Evangelist Mark presents the calling of the Twelve: Jesus "went up into the hills, and *called* to him those *whom he desired;* and *they came* to him" (*Mk* 3:13). On the one hand, we have the completely free decision of Jesus; on the other, the "coming" of the Twelve, their "following" Jesus.

This is the constant paradigm, the fundamental datum of every vocation: whether of Prophets, Apostles, priests, religious, the lay faithful—of everyone.

First of all, indeed in a prevenient and decisive way, comes *the free and gracious intervention of God who calls.* It is God who takes the initiative in the call. This was, for example, the experience of the Prophet Jeremiah: "Now the word of the Lord came to me saying, 'Before I formed you in the womb I knew you, and before you were born I consecrated you; I appointed you a prophet to the nations'" (*Jer* 1:4-5). The same truth is presented by the Apostle Paul, who roots every vocation in the eternal election in Christ, made "before

94

the foundation of the world" and "according to the purpose of his will" (*Eph* 1:4-5). The absolute primacy of grace in vocation is most perfectly proclaimed in the words of Jesus: "You did not choose me, but I chose you and appointed you that you should go and bear fruit and that your fruit should abide" (*Jn* 15:16).

If the priestly vocation bears unequivocal witness to the primacy of grace, God's free and sovereign decision to call man calls for total respect. It cannot be forced in the slightest by any human ambition, and it cannot be replaced by any human decision. Vocation is a gift of God's grace and never a human right, such that "one can never consider priestly life as a simply human affair, nor the mission of the minister as a simply personal project".[101] Every claim or presumption on the part of those called is thus radically excluded (cf. *Heb* 5:4ff.). Their entire heart and spirit should be filled with an amazed and deeply felt gratitude, an unshakeable trust and hope, because those who have been called know that they are rooted not in their own strength but in the unconditional faithfulness of God who calls.

"He called to him those whom he desired; and they came to him" (*Mk* 3:13). This "coming", which is the same as "following" Jesus, expresses the free response of the Twelve to the Master's call. We see it in the case of Peter and Andrew: "And he said to them, 'Follow me and I will make you fishers of men.' Immediately they left their

---

[101] *Angelus* (3 December 1989), 2: *Insegnamenti* XII/2 (1989), 1417.

nets and followed him" (*Mt* 4:19-20). The experience of James and John was exactly the same (cf. *Mt* 4:21-22). And so it is always: in vocation there shine out at the same time God's gracious love and the highest possible exaltation of man's freedom: the freedom of following God's call and entrusting oneself to him.

In effect, grace and freedom are not opposed. On the contrary, grace enlivens and sustains human freedom, setting it free from the slavery of sin (cf. *Jn* 8:34-36), healing it and elevating it in its ability to be open to receiving God's gift. And if we cannot in any way minimize the absolutely gratuitous initiative of God who calls, neither can we in any way minimize the serious responsibility which man faces in the challenge of his freedom. And so when he hears Jesus's invitation to "come, follow me" the rich young man refuses, a sign—albeit only a negative sign—of his freedom: "At that saying his countenance fell, and he went away sorrowful; for he had great possessions" (*Mk* 10:22).

Freedom, therefore, *is essential to vocation,* a freedom which when it gives a positive response appears as a deep personal adherence, as a loving gift, or rather as a gift given back to the Giver who is God who calls, an oblation: "The call—Paul VI once said—is as extensive as the response. There cannot be vocations, unless they be free; that is, unless they be spontaneous offerings of oneself, conscious, generous, total... Oblations, we call them: here lies in practice the heart of the matter... It is the humble and penetrating voice of

Christ, who says, today, as yesterday, and even more than yesterday: come. Freedom reaches its supreme foundation: precisely that of oblation, of generosity, of sacrifice".[102]

The free oblation, which constitutes the intimate and most precious core of man's response to God who calls, finds its incomparable model, indeed its living root, in the most free oblation which Jesus Christ, the first of those called, made to the Father's will: "Consequently, when Christ came into the world, he said, 'Sacrifices and offerings you have not desired, but a body have you prepared for me... Then I said, Lo, I have come to do your will, O God'" (*Heb* 10:5, 7).

The creature who more than any other has lived the full truth of vocation is Mary the Virgin Mother, and she did so in intimate communion with Christ: no one has responded with a love greater than hers to the immense love of God.[103]

37.   "At that saying his countenance fell, and he went away sorrowful; for he had great possessions" (*Mk* 10:22). The rich young man in the Gospel who did not follow Jesus's call reminds us of the obstacles preventing or eliminating man's free response: material goods are not the only things that can shut the human heart to the values of the Spirit and the radical demands of the Kingdom of God; certain social and cultural conditions of our day can also present many threats and can

---

[102] *Message for the Fifth World Day of Prayer for Priestly Vocations* (19 April 1968): *Insegnamenti* VI (1968), 134-135.
[103] Cf. *Propositio* 5.

impose distorted and false visions about the true nature of vocation, making it difficult, if not impossible, to embrace or even to understand it.

Many people have such a general and confused idea of God that their religiosity becomes a religiosity without God, where God's will is seen as an immutable and unavoidable fate to which man has to bend and resign himself in a totally passive manner. But this is not the face of God which Jesus Christ came to reveal to us: God is truly a Father who with an eternal and prevenient love calls human beings and opens up with them a marvellous and permanent dialogue, inviting them, as his children, to share his own divine life. It is true that if human beings have an erroneous vision of God they cannot even recognize the truth about themselves, and thus they will be unable to perceive or live their vocation in its genuine value: vocation will be felt only as a crushing burden imposed upon them.

Certain distorted ideas regarding man, sometimes backed up by specious philosophical or "scientific" theories, also sometimes lead people to consider their own existence and freedom as totally determined and conditioned by external factors, of an educational, psychological, cultural or environmental type. In other cases, freedom is understood in terms of total autonomy, the sole and indisputable basis for personal choices, and effectively as self-affirmation at any cost. But these ways of thinking make it impossible to understand and live one's vocation as a free dialogue of love, which arises from the communication of God to man and ends in the sincere self-giving.

In the present context there is also a certain tendency to view the bond between human beings and God in an individualistic and self-centred way, as if God's call reached the individual by a direct route, without in any way passing through the community. Its purpose is held to be the benefit, or the very salvation, of the individual called and not a total dedication to God in the service of the community. We thus find another very deep and at the same time subtle threat which makes it impossible to recognize and accept joyfully the ecclesial dimension which naturally marks every Christian vocation, and the priestly vocation in particular: as the Council reminds us, priestly ministry acquires its genuine meaning and attains to its fullest truth in serving and in fostering the growth of the Christian community and the common priesthood of the faithful.[104]

The cultural context which we have just recalled, and which affects Christians themselves and especially young people, helps us to understand the spread of the crisis of priestly vocations, a crisis that is rooted in and accompanied by even more radical crises of faith. The Synod Fathers made this very point when recognizing that the crisis of vocations to the priesthood has deep roots in the cultural environment and in the outlook and practical behaviour of Christians.[105]

[104] Cf. Dogmatic Constitution on the Church *Lumen Gentium,* 10; Decree on the Ministry and Life of Priests *Presbyterorum Ordinis*, 12.
[105] Cf. *Propositio* 13.

Hence the urgent need that the Church's pastoral work in promoting vocations be aimed decisively and primarily towards restoring a "Christian mentality", one built on faith and sustained by it. More than ever, what is now needed is an evangelization which never tires of pointing to the true face of God, the Father who calls each one of us in Jesus Christ, and to the genuine meaning of human freedom as the principle driving force behind the responsible gift of oneself. Only thus will the indispensable foundations be laid, so that every vocation, including the priestly vocation, will be perceived for what it really is, loved in its beauty and lived out with total dedication and deep joy.

CONTENT AND METHODS OF PASTORAL WORK FOR PROMOTING VOCATIONS

38.   Certainly a vocation is a fathomless mystery involving the relationship established by God with human beings in their absolute uniqueness, a mystery perceived and heard as a call which awaits a response in the depths of one's conscience, which is "man's most secret core, and his sanctuary. There he is alone with God whose voice echoes in his depths".[106] But this does not eliminate the communitarian and in particular the ecclesial dimension of vocation. The Church is also truly

---

[106] SECOND VATICAN ECUMENICAL COUNCIL, Pastoral Constitution on the Church in the Modern World *Gaudium et Spes*, 16.

present and at work in the vocation of every priest.

In her service to the priestly vocation and its development, that is, in the birth, discernment and care of each vocation, the Church can look for her model to Andrew, one of the first two disciples who set out to follow Jesus. Andrew himself told his brother what had happened to him: " 'We have found the Messiah' (which means Christ)" (*Jn* 1:41). His account of this "discovery" opened the way to a meeting: *"He brought him to Jesus"* (*Jn* 1:42). There can be no doubt about the absolutely free initiative nor about the sovereign decision of Jesus. It is Jesus who calls Simon and gives him a new name: "Jesus looked at him, and said, 'So you are Simon the son of John? You shall be called Cephas' (which means Peter)" (*Jn* 1:42). But Andrew also acted with initiative: he arranged his brother's meeting with Jesus.

"He brought him to Jesus". In a way, this is the heart of all the Church's pastoral work on behalf of vocations, in which she cares for the birth and growth of vocations, making use of the gifts and responsibilities, of the charisms and ministry she has received from Christ and his Spirit. The Church, as a priestly, prophetic and kingly people, is committed to foster and to serve the birth and maturing of priestly vocations through her prayer and sacramental life, by her proclamation of the Word and by education in the faith, by her example and witness of charity.

The Church, in her dignity and responsibility as a priestly people, possesses in prayer and in the

101

celebration of the *Liturgy the essential and primary stages of her pastoral work for vocations.* Indeed, Christian prayer, nourished by the word of God, creates an ideal environment where each individual can discover the truth of his own being and the identity of the personal and unrepeatable life project which the Father entrusts to him. It is therefore necessary to educate boys and young men so that they will become faithful to prayer and meditation on God's word: in silence and listening, they will be able to perceive the Lord who is calling them to the priesthood, and be able to follow that call promptly and generously.

The Church should daily take up Jesus' persuasive and demanding invitation to "pray the Lord of the harvest to send out labourers into his harvest" (*Mt* 9:38). Obedient to Christ's command, the Church first of all makes a humble profession of faith: in praying for vocations, conscious of her urgent need of them for her very life and mission, she acknowledges that they are a gift of God and, as such, must be asked for by a ceaseless and trusting prayer of petition. This prayer, the pivot of all pastoral work for vocations, is required not only of individuals but of entire ecclesial communities. There can be no doubt about the importance of individual initiatives of prayer, of special times set apart for such prayer, beginning with the World Day of Prayer for Vocations, and of the explicit commitment of persons and groups particularly concerned with the problem of priestly vocations. Today the prayerful expectation of new vocations should become an ever more continual and widespread habit within the entire Christian community and in every one of its parts. Thus it will be possible to re-live the experience of the Apostles in the Upper Room who, in union with Mary, prayerfully awaited the outpouring of the Spirit (cf. *Acts* 1:14), who will not fail to raise up once again in the People of God "worthy ministers for the altar, ardent but gentle proclaimers of the Gospel".[107]

In addition, the Liturgy, as the summit and source of the Church's existence [108] and in particular of all Christian prayer, plays an influential and indispensable role in the pastoral work of promoting vocations. The Liturgy is a living experience of God's gift and a great school for learning how to respond to his call. As such, every liturgical celebration, and especially the Eucharist, reveals to us the true face of God and grants us a share in the Paschal Mystery, in the "hour" for which Jesus came into the world and towards which he freely and willingly made his way in obedience to the Father's call (cf. *Jn* 13:1). It shows us the Church as a priestly people and a community structured in the variety and complementarity of its charisms and vocations. The redemptive sacrifice of Christ, which the Church celebrates in mystery, accords a particular value to suffering endured in union with the Lord Jesus. The Synod Fathers invited us never to forget that "through the offering of suf-

---

[107] ROMAN MISSAL, Collect of the Mass for Vocations to Holy Orders.
[108] Cf. SECOND VATICAN ECUMENICAL COUNCIL, Constitution on the Sacred Liturgy *Sacrosanctum Concilium*, 10.

ferings, which are so frequent in human life, the Christian who is ill offers himself as a victim to God, in the image of Christ, who has consecrated himself for us all" (cf. *Jn* 17:19) and that "the offering of sufferings for this intention is a great help in fostering vocations".[109]

39.   In carrying out her prophetic role, the Church feels herself irrevocably committed to the task of *proclaiming and witnessing to the Christian meaning of vocation,* or as we might say, to "the Gospel of vocation". Here too, she feels the urgency of the Apostle's exclamation: "Woe to me if I do not preach the gospel!" (*1 Cor* 9:16). This admonishment rings out especially for us who are pastors but, together with us, it touches all educators in the Church. Preaching and catechesis must always show their intrinsic vocational dimension: the word of God enlightens believers to appreciate life as a response to God's call and leads them to embrace in faith the gift of a personal vocation.

But all this, however important and even essential, is not enough: we need a "direct preaching on the mystery of vocation in the Church, on the value of the ministerial priesthood, on God's people's urgent need of it".[110] A properly structured catechesis, directed to all the members of the Church, in addition to dissipating doubts and countering one-sided or distorted ideas about priestly ministry, will open believers' hearts to expect the gift and create favourable conditions for

[109] *Propositio* 15.
[110] *Ibid.*

the birth of new vocations. The time has come to speak courageously about priestly life as a priceless gift and a splendid and privileged form of Christian living. Educators, and priests in particular, should not be afraid to set forth explicitly and forcefully the priestly vocation as a real possibility for those young people who demonstrate the necessary gifts and talents. There should be no fear that one is thereby conditioning them or limiting their freedom; quite the contrary, a clear invitation, made at the right time, can be decisive in eliciting from young people a free and genuine response. Besides, the history of the Church and that of many individual priests whose vocations blossomed at a young age bear ample witness to how providential the presence and conversation of a priest can be: not only his words, but his very presence, a concrete and joyful witness which can raise questions and lead to decisions, even definitive ones.

40. As a kingly people, the Church sees herself rooted in and enlivened by "the law of the Spirit of life" (*Rom* 8:2), which is essentially the royal law of charity (cf. *Jas* 2:8) or the perfect law of freedom (cf. *Jas* 1:25). Therefore, the Church fulfils her mission when *she guides every member of the faithful to discover and live his or her own vocation in freedom and to bring it to fulfilment in charity*.

In carrying out her educational role, the Church aims with special concern at developing in children, adolescents and young men a desire and a will to follow Jesus Christ in a total and attractive way. This educational work, while addressed to the Christian community as such, must also be aimed at the individual person: indeed, God with his call reaches the heart of each individual, and the Spirit, who abides deep within each disciple (cf. *1 Jn* 3:24), gives himself to each Christian with different charisms and special signs. Each one, therefore, must be helped to embrace the gift entrusted to him as a completely unique person, and to hear the words which the Spirit of God personally addresses to him.

From this point of view, the pastoral work of promoting vocations to the priesthood will also be able to find expression in a firm and encouraging invitation to *spiritual direction.* It is necessary to rediscover the great tradition of personal spiritual guidance which has always brought great and precious fruits to the Church's life. In certain cases and under precise conditions this work can be assisted, but not replaced, by forms of analysis or psychological help.[111] Children, adolescents and young men are invited to discover and appreciate the gift of spiritual direction, to look for it and experience it, and to ask for it with trusting insistence from those who are their educators in the faith. Priests, for their part, should be the first to devote time and energies to this work of education and personal spiritual guidance: they will never regret having neglected or put in second place

---

[111] Cf. *C.I.C.*, can. 220: "It is not lawful for anyone (...) to violate the right which each person has of defending his own privacy"; cf. can. 642.

so many other things which are themselves good and useful, if this proved necessary for them to be faithful to their ministry as cooperators of the Spirit in enlightening and guiding those who have been called.

The aim of education for a Christian is to attain the "stature of the fullness of Christ" (*Eph* 4:13) under the influence of the Spirit. This happens when, imitating and sharing Christ's charity, a person turns his entire life into an act of loving service (cf. *Jn* 13:14-15), offering to God a spiritual worship acceptable to him (cf. *Rom* 12:1) and giving himself to his brothers and sisters. *The service of love is the fundamental meaning of every vocation,* and it finds a specific expression in the priestly vocation. Indeed, a priest is called to live out, as radically as possible, the pastoral charity of Jesus, the love of the Good Shepherd who "lays down his life for the sheep" (*Jn* 10:11).

Consequently, an authentic pastoral work on behalf of vocations will never tire of training boys, adolescents and young men to appreciate commitment, the meaning of free service, the value of sacrifice and unconditional self-giving. In this context it is easy to see the great value of forms of volunteer work, which so many young people are growing to appreciate. If volunteer work is inspired by the Gospel values, capable of training people to discern true needs, lived with dedication and faithfulness each day, open to the possibility of a total commitment in consecrated life and nourished in prayer, then it will be more readily able to sustain a life of disinterested and free commitment and will make the one involved in it more sensitive to the voice of God who may be calling him to the priesthood. Unlike the rich young man, the person involved in volunteer work would be able to accept the invitation lovingly addressed to him by Jesus (cf. *Mk* 10:21); and he would be able to accept it because his only wealth now consists in giving himself to others and in "losing" his life.

WE ARE ALL RESPONSIBLE FOR PRIESTLY VOCATIONS

41.   The priestly vocation is a gift from God. It is undoubtedly a great good for the person who is its first recipient. But it is also a gift to the Church as a whole, a benefit to her life and mission. The Church, therefore, is called to safeguard this gift, to esteem it and love it. She is responsible for the birth and development of priestly vocations. Consequently, the pastoral work of promoting vocations has as its active agents, as its protagonists, the ecclesial community as such, in its various expressions: from the universal Church to the particular Church and, by analogy, from the particular Church to each of its parishes and to every part of the People of God.

There is an urgent need, especially nowadays, for a more widespread and deeply felt conviction that *all the members of the Church, without exception, have the grace and responsibility to look after vocations.* The Second Vatican Council was quite explicit in this regard: "The duty of fostering vocations falls on the whole Christian community,

108

and they should discharge it principally by living full Christian lives".[112] Only on the basis of this conviction will pastoral work on behalf of vocations be able to show its truly ecclesial aspect, develop a harmonious plan of action, and make use of specific agencies and appropriate instruments of communion and corresponsibility.

The first responsibility for the pastoral work of promoting priestly vocations lies with the *Bishop*,[113] who is called to be the first to exercise this responsibility, even though he can and must call upon many others to cooperate with him. As the father and friend of his presbyterate, it falls primarily to the Bishop to be concerned about "giving continuity" to the priestly charism and ministry, bringing it new forces by the laying on of hands. He will be actively concerned to ensure that the vocational dimension is always present in the whole range of ordinary pastoral work, and that it is fully integrated and practically identified with it. It is his duty to foster and coordinate various initiatives on behalf of vocations.[114]

The Bishop can rely above all on the cooperation of his presbyterate. All its *priests* are united to him and share his responsibility in seeking and fostering priestly vocations. Indeed, as the Council states, "it is the priests' part as instructors of the people in the faith to see to it that each member

---

[112] Decree on Priestly Formation *Optatam Totius*, 2.
[113] Cf. SECOND VATICAN ECUMENICAL COUNCIL, Decree on the Pastoral Office of Bishops in the Church *Christus Dominus*, 15.
[114] Cf. SECOND VATICAN ECUMENICAL COUNCIL, Decree on Priestly Formation *Optatam Totius*, 2.

of the faithful shall be led in the Holy Spirit to the full development of his own vocation".[115] "This duty belongs to the very nature of the priestly ministry which makes the priest share in the concern of the whole Church lest labourers should ever be wanting to the People of God here on earth".[116] The very life of priests, their unconditional dedication to God's flock, their witness of loving service to the Lord and to his Church—a witness marked by free acceptance of the Cross in the spirit of hope and Easter joy—their fraternal unity and zeal for the evangelization of the world are the first and most convincing factor in the growth of vocations.[117]

A very special responsibility falls upon the *Christian family,* which by virtue of the Sacrament of Matrimony shares in its own unique way in the educational mission of the Church, Teacher and Mother. As the Synod Fathers wrote: "the Christian family, which is truly a 'domestic church' (*Lumen Gentium,* 11), has always offered and continues to offer favourable conditions for the birth of vocations. Since the reality of the Christian family is endangered nowadays, much importance should be given to pastoral work on behalf of the family, in order that the families themselves, generously accepting the gift of human life, may be 'as it were, a first seminary' (*Optatam Totius,* 2) in which children can acquire from the beginning an

---

[115] Decree on the Ministry and Life of Priests *Presbyterorum Ordinis,* 6.

[116] *Ibid.,* 11.

[117] Cf. SECOND VATICAN ECUMENICAL COUNCIL, Decree on Priestly Formation *Optatam Totius,* 2.

110

awareness of piety and prayer and of love for the Church".[118] Following upon and in harmony with the work of parents and the family, is the *school,* which is called to live its identity as an "educating community", also by providing a correct understanding of the dimension of vocation as an innate and fundamental value of the human person. In this sense, if it is endowed with a Christian spirit (either by a significant presence of members of the Church in state schools, following the laws of each country, or above all in the case of the Catholic school), it can infuse "in the hearts of boys and young men a desire to do God's will in that state in life which is most suitable to each person, and never excluding the vocation to the priestly ministry".[119]

The *lay faithful* also, and particularly catechists, teachers, educators and youth ministers, each with his or her own resources and style, have great importance in the pastoral work of promoting priestly vocations: the more they inculcate a deep appreciation of young people's vocation and mission in the Church, the more they will be able to recognize the unique value of the priestly vocation and mission.

With regard to diocesan and parish communities, special appreciation and encouragement should be given to *groups which promote vocations,* whose members make an important contribution by prayer and sufferings offered up for priestly and religious vocations, as well as by moral and material support.

[118] *Propositio* 14.
[119] *Propositio* 15.

111

We should also remember the numerous *groups, movements and associations of lay faithful* whom the Holy Spirit raises up and fosters in the Church with a view to a more missionary Christian presence in the world. These various groupings of lay people are proving a particularly fertile field for the manifestation of vocations to consecrated life, and are truly environments in which vocations can be encouraged and can grow. Many young people, in and through these groupings, have heard the Lord's call to follow him along the path of priestly ministry [120] and have responded with a generosity that is reassuring. These groupings, therefore, are to be utilized well, so that in communion with the whole Church and for the sake of her growth they may make their proper contribution to the development of the pastoral work of promoting vocations.

The various elements and members of the Church involved in the pastoral work of promoting vocations will make their work more effective insofar as they stimulate the ecclesial community as such, starting with the parish, to sense that the problem of priestly vocations cannot in any way be delegated to some "official" group (priests in general and the priests working in the seminary in particular), for inasmuch as it is "a vital problem which lies at the very heart of the Church", [121] it should be at the heart of the love which each Christian feels for the Church.

---

[120] Cf. *Propositio* 16.
[121] *Message for the 22nd World Day of Prayer for Priestly Vocations* (13 April 1985), 1: *AAS* 77 (1985), 982.

CHAPTER V

HE APPOINTED TWELVE
TO BE WITH HIM

THE FORMATION OF CANDIDATES
FOR THE PRIESTHOOD

FOLLOWING CHRIST AS THE APOSTLES DID

42.   "And he went up on the mountain, and
called to him those whom he desired; and they
came to him. And he appointed twelve, to be with
him, and to be sent out to preach and have
authority to cast out demons" (*Mk* 3:13-15).

"To be with him": it is not difficult to find in
these words a reference to Jesus's "accompanying" the Apostles for the sake of their vocation.
After calling them and before he sends them out,
indeed in order to be able to send them out to
preach, Jesus asks them to set aside a "period
of time" for formation. The aim of this time is to
develop a relationship of deep communion and
friendship with himself. In this time they receive
the benefit of a catechesis that is deeper than the
teaching he gives to the people (cf. *Mt* 13:11); also
he wishes them to be witnesses of his silent prayer
to the Father (cf. *Jn* 17:1-26; *Lk* 22:39-45).

In her care for priestly vocations the Church

113

in every age draws her inspiration from Christ's example. There have been, and to some extent there still are, *many different practical forms* according to which the Church has been involved in the pastoral care of vocations. Her task is not only to discern but also to "accompany" priestly vocations. But *the spirit* which must inspire and sustain her *remains the same:* that of bringing to the priesthood only those who have been called, and to bring them adequately trained, namely, with a conscious and free response of adherence and involvement of their whole person with Jesus Christ who calls them to intimacy of life with him and to share in his mission of salvation. In this sense, the "seminary" in its different forms, and analogously the "house" of formation for religious priests, more than a place, a material space, should be a spiritual place, a way of life, an atmosphere that fosters and ensures a process of formation, so that the person who is called to the priesthood by God may become, with the Sacrament of Orders, a living image of Jesus Christ, Head and Shepherd of the Church. In their *Final Message* the Synod Fathers have grasped in a direct and deep way the original and specific meaning of the formation of candidates for the priesthood, when they say that "To live in the seminary, which is a school of the Gospel, means to follow Christ as the Apostles did. You are led by Christ into the service of God the Father and of all people, under the guidance of the Holy Spirit. Thus you become more like Christ the Good Shepherd in order better to serve the Church and the world as a priest. In preparing for the priesthood we learn how to respond from the heart to Christ's basic question: 'Do you love me?' (*Jn* 21:15). For the future priest the answer can only mean total self-giving".[122]

What needs to be done is to transfer this spirit, which can never be lacking in the Church, to the social, psychological, political and cultural conditions of the world today, conditions which are so varied and complex, as the Synod Fathers have confirmed, bearing in mind the different particular Churches. The Fathers, with words expressing thoughtful concern but at the same time great hope, have shown awareness of and reflected at length on the efforts going on in all their Churches to identify and update methods of training candidates for the priesthood.

This present Exhortation seeks to gather the results of the work of the Synod, setting out some *established points,* indicating some *essential goals,* making available to all the *wealth of experiences and training programmes* which have already been tried and found worthwhile. In this Exhortation we consider *"initial" formation* and *"ongoing" formation* separately, but without forgetting that they are closely linked and that as a result they should become one sole organic journey of Christian and priestly living. The Exhortation looks at the different *areas* of *formation*—the *human, spiritual, intellectual and pastoral* areas—as well as the *settings*

---

[122] *Message of the Synod Fathers to the People of God* (28 October 1990), IV: *loc. cit.*

and the *persons responsible* for the formation of candidates for the priesthood.

I. THE AREAS OF PRIESTLY FORMATION

Human formation, the basis of all priestly formation

43. "The whole work of priestly formation would be deprived of its necessary foundation if it lacked a suitable human formation".[123] This statement by the Synod Fathers expresses not only a fact which reason brings to our consideration every day and which experience confirms, but a requirement which has a deeper and specific motivation in the very nature of the priest and his ministry. The priest, who is called to be a "living image" of Jesus Christ, Head and Shepherd of the Church, should seek to reflect in himself, as far as possible, the human perfection which shines forth in the Incarnate Son of God and which is reflected with particular liveliness in his attitudes towards others as we see narrated in the Gospels. The ministry of the priest is, certainly, to proclaim the Word, to celebrate the Sacraments, to guide the Christian community in charity "in the name and in the person of Christ", but all this he does dealing always and only with individual human beings: "Every high priest chosen from among men is appointed to act on behalf of men in relation to God" (*Heb* 5:1). So we see that the human formation of the priest shows its special im-

---

[123] *Propositio* 21.

116

portance when related to the receivers of the mission: in order that his ministry may be humanly as credible and acceptable as possible, it is important that the priest should mould his human personality in such a way that it becomes a bridge and not an obstacle for others in their meeting with Jesus Christ the Redeemer of man. It is necessary that, following the example of Jesus who "knew what was in man" (*Jn* 2:25, cf. 8:3-11), the priest should be able to know the depths of the human heart, to perceive difficulties and problems, to make meeting and dialogue easy, to create trust and cooperation, to express serene and objective judgments.

Future priests should therefore cultivate a series of human qualities, not only out of proper and due growth and realization of self, but also with a view to the ministry. These qualities are needed for them to be balanced people, strong and free, capable of bearing the weight of pastoral responsibilities. They need to be educated to love the truth, to be loyal, to respect every person, to have a sense of justice, to be true to their word, to be genuinely compassionate, to be men of integrity and, especially, to be balanced in judgment and behaviour.[124] A simple and demanding programme for this human formation can be found in the words of the Apostle Paul to the Philippians:

---

[124] Cf. SECOND VATICAN ECUMENICAL COUNCIL, Decree on Priestly Formation *Optatam Totius,* 11; Decree on the Ministry and Life of Priests *Presbyterorum Ordinis,* 3; SACRED CONGREGATION FOR CATHOLIC EDUCATION, *Ratio Fundamentalis Institutionis Sacerdotalis,* (6 January 1970), 51: *loc. cit.,* 356-357.

"whatever is true, whatever is honourable, whatever is just, whatever is pure, whatever is lovely, whatever is gracious, if there is any excellence, if there is anything worthy of praise, think about these things" (*Phil* 4:8). It is interesting to note that Paul, precisely in these profoundly human qualities, presents himself as a model to his faithful, for he goes on to say: "What you have learned and received and heard and seen in me, do" (*Phil* 4:9).

Of special importance is the capacity to relate to others. This is truly fundamental for a person who is called to be responsible for a community and to be a "man of communion". This demands that the priest not be arrogant, or quarrelsome, but affable, hospitable, sincere in his words and heart, prudent and discreet, generous and ready to serve, capable of opening himself to clear and brotherly relationships and of encouraging the same in others, and quick to understand, forgive and console [125] (see also *1 Tim* 3:1-5; *Tit* 1:7-9). People today are often trapped in situations of standardization and loneliness, especially in large urban centres, and they become ever more appreciative of the value of communion. Today this is one of the most eloquent signs and one of the most effective ways of transmitting the Gospel message.

In this context affective maturity, which is the result of an education in true and responsible love,

[125] Cf. *Propositio* 21.

is a significant and decisive factor in the formation of candidates for the priesthood.

44. *Affective maturity* presupposes an awareness that love has a central role in human life. In fact, as I have written in the Encyclical *Redemptor Hominis,* "Man cannot live without love. He remains a being that is incomprehensible for himself, his life is meaningless, if love is not revealed to him, if he does not encounter love, if he does not experience it and make it his own, if he does not participate intimately in it".[126]

We are speaking of a love that involves the entire person, in all his aspects, physical, psychic and spiritual, and which is expressed in the "nuptial meaning" of the human body, thanks to which a person gives himself to another and takes the other to himself. A properly understood sexual education leads to understanding and realizing this "truth" about human love. We need to be aware that there is a widespread social and cultural atmosphere which "largely reduces human sexuality to the level of something commonplace, since it interprets and lives it in a reductive and impoverished way by linking it solely with the body and with selfish pleasure".[127] Sometimes the very family situations in which priestly vocations arise will display not a few weaknesses and at times even serious failings.

[126] Encyclical Letter *Redemptor Hominis* (4 March 1979), 10: *AAS* 71 (1979), 274.
[127] Apostolic Exhortation *Familiaris Consortio* (22 November 1981), 37: *loc. cit.,* 128.

In such a context, an *education for sexuality* becomes more difficult but also more urgent. It should be truly and fully personal and therefore should present chastity in a manner that shows appreciation and love for it as a "virtue that develops a person's authentic maturity and makes him or her capable of respecting and fostering the 'nuptial meaning' of the body".[128]

Education for responsible love and the affective maturity of the person are totally necessary for those who, like the priest, are called to *celibacy,* that is, to offer with the grace of the Spirit and the free response of one's own will the whole of one's love and care to Jesus Christ and to his Church. In view of the commitment to celibacy, affective maturity should bring to human relationships of serene friendship and deep brotherliness a strong, lively and personal love for Jesus Christ. As the Synod Fathers have written, "A love for Christ, which overflows into a dedication to everyone, is of the greatest importance in developing affective maturity. Thus the candidate, who is called to celibacy, will find in affective maturity a firm support to live chastity in faithfulness and joy".[129]

Since the charism of celibacy, even when it is genuine and has proved itself, leaves man's affections and his instinctive impulses intact, candidates to the priesthood need an affective maturity which is prudent, able to renounce anything that is a threat to it, vigilant over both body and spirit,

[128] *Ibid.*
[129] *Propositio* 21.

and capable of esteem and respect in interpersonal relationships between men and women. A precious help can be given by a suitable education to true *friendship,* following the image of the bonds of fraternal affection which Christ himself lived on earth (cf. *Jn* 11:5).

Human maturity, and in particular affective maturity, requires a clear and strong *training in freedom* which expresses itself in convinced and heartfelt obedience to the "truth" of one's own being, to the "meaning" of one's own existence, that is to the "sincere gift of self" as the way and fundamental content of the authentic realization of self.[130] Thus understood, freedom requires the person to be truly master of himself, determined to fight and overcome the different forms of selfishness and individualism which threaten the life of each one, ready to open out to others, generous in dedication and service to one's neighbour. This is important for the response that will have to be given to the vocation, and in particular to the priestly vocation, and for faithfulness to it and to the commitments connected with it, even in times of difficulty. On this educational journey towards a mature, responsible freedom the community life of the Seminary can provide help.[131]

Intimately connected with formation to responsible freedom is *education of the moral conscience.* Such education calls from the depths of one's own "self" obedience to moral obligations

---

[130] Cf. SECOND VATICAN ECUMENICAL COUNCIL, Pastoral Constitution on the Church in the Modern World *Gaudium et Spes,* 24.
[131] Cf. *Propositio* 21.

and at the same time reveals the deep meaning of such obedience. It is a conscious and free response, and therefore a loving response, to God's demands, to God's love. "The human maturity of the priest—the Synod Fathers write—should include especially the formation of his conscience. In order that the candidate may faithfully meet his obligations with regard to God and the Church and wisely guide the consciences of the faithful, he should become accustomed to listening to the voice of God, who speaks to him in his heart, and to adhere with love and constancy to his will".[132]

SPIRITUAL FORMATION: IN COMMUNION WITH GOD AND IN SEARCH OF CHRIST

45.   Human formation, when it is carried out in the context of an anthropology which is open to the full truth regarding man, leads to and finds its completion in spiritual formation. Every man, as God's creature who has been redeemed by Christ's blood, is called to be reborn "of water and the Spirit" (*Jn* 3:5) and to become a "son in the Son". In this wonderful plan of God is to be found the basis of the essentially religious dimension of the human person, which moreover can be grasped and recognized by reason itself: man is open to transcendence, to the absolute; he has a heart which is restless until it rests in the Lord.[133]

---

[132] *Propositio* 22.
[133] Cf. SAINT AUGUSTINE, *Confessions,* 1,1: *CSEL* 33,1.

The educational process of a spiritual life, seen as a relationship and communion with God, derives and develops from this fundamental and irrepressible religious need. In the light of revelation and Christian experience, spiritual formation possesses the unmistakable originality which derives from evangelical "newness". Indeed, it "is the work of the Holy Spirit and engages a person in his totality. It introduces him to a deep communion with Jesus Christ, the Good Shepherd, and leads to the total submission of one's life to the Spirit, in a filial attitude towards the Father and a trustful attachment to the Church. Spiritual formation has its roots in the experience of the Cross, which in deep communion leads to the totality of the Paschal Mystery". [134]

Spiritual formation, as we have just seen, is applicable to all the faithful. Nevertheless, it should be structured according to the meanings and connotations which derive from the identity of the priest and his ministry. And just as for all the faithful spiritual formation is central and unifies their being and living as Christians, that is, as new creatures in Christ who walk in the Spirit, so too for every priest his spiritual formation is the core which unifies and gives life to his *being* a priest and his *acting as* a priest. In this context, the Synod Fathers state that "without spiritual formation pastoral formation would be left without

---

[134] SYNOD OF BISHOPS, 8th Ordinary General Assembly, "The Formation of Priests in the Circumstances of the Present Day", *Instrumentum laboris*, 30.

foundation" [135] and that spiritual formation is "an extremely important element of a priest's education". [136]

The essential content of spiritual formation specifically leading towards the priesthood is well expressed in the Council's Decree *Optatam Totius*: "Spiritual formation (...) should be conducted in such a way that the students may learn to live in intimate and unceasing union with God the Father through his Son Jesus Christ, in the Holy Spirit. Those who are to take on the likeness of Christ the priest by sacred ordination should form the habit of drawing close to him as friends in every detail of their lives. They should live his Paschal Mystery in such a way that they will know how to initiate into it the people committed to their charge. They should be taught to seek Christ in faithful meditation on the word of God and in active participation in the sacred mysteries of the Church, especially the Eucharist and the Divine Office, to seek him in the Bishop by whom they are sent and in the people to whom they are sent, especially the poor, little children, the weak, sinners and unbelievers. With the confidence of sons they should love and reverence the most Blessed Virgin Mary, who was given as a mother to the disciple by Jesus Christ as he was dying on the Cross". [137]

---

[135] *Propositio* 22.
[136] *Propositio* 23.
[137] Decree on Priestly Formation *Optatam Totius*, 8.

124

46.   This text from the Council deserves our careful and loving meditation, out of which we will easily be able to outline some fundamental values and demands of the spiritual path trodden by the candidate for the priesthood.

First, there is the value and demand of *"living intimately united" to Jesus Christ.* Our union with the Lord Jesus, which has its roots in Baptism and is nourished with the Eucharist, has to express itself and be radically renewed each day. Intimate communion with the Blessed Trinity, that is, the new life of grace which makes us children of God, constitutes the "novelty" of the believer, a novelty which involves both his being and his acting. It constitutes the "mystery" of Christian existence which is under the influence of the Spirit: it should, as a result, constitute the ethos of Christian living. Jesus has taught us this marvellous reality of Christian living, which is also the heart of spiritual life, with his allegory of the vine and the branches: "I am the true vine, and my Father is the vinedresser... Abide in me, and I in you. As the branch cannot bear fruit by itself, unless it abides in the vine, neither can you, unless you abide in me. I am the vine, you are the branches. He who abides in me, and I in him, he it is that bears much fruit, for apart from me you can do nothing" (*Jn* 15:1, 4-5).

There are spiritual and religious values present in today's culture, and man, notwithstanding appearances to the contrary, cannot help but hunger and thirst for God. However, the Christian religion is often regarded as just one religion among many or reduced to nothing more than a social ethic at the service of man. As a result its amazing novelty in human history is quite often not apparent. It is a "mystery", the event of the coming of the Son of God who becomes man and gives to those who welcome him the "power to become children of God" (*Jn* 1:12). It is the proclamation, nay the gift of a personal covenant of love and life between God and man. Only if future priests, through a suitable spiritual formation, have become deeply aware and have increasingly experienced this "mystery" will they be able to communicate this amazing and blessed message to others (cf. *1 Jn* 1:1-4).

The Council text, while taking account of the absolute transcendence of the Christian mystery, describes the communion of future priests with Jesus in *terms of friendship*. And indeed it is not an absurdity for man to aim at this, for it is the priceless gift of Christ, who said to his Apostles: "No longer do I call you servants, for the servant does not know what the master is doing; but I have called you friends, for all that I have heard from my Father I have made known to you" (*Jn* 15:15).

The Council text then points out a second great spiritual value: *the search for Jesus.* "They should be taught to seek Christ". This, along with the *quaerere Deum* (the search for God), is a classical theme of Christian spirituality. It has a specific application in the context of the calling of the Apostles. When John tells the story of the way the first two disciples followed Christ, he highlights this "search". It is Jesus himself who asks the question: "What do you seek?" And the two reply: "Rabbi, where are you staying?" The Evangelist continues: "He said to them, 'Come and see.' They came and saw where he was staying; and they stayed with him that day" (*Jn* 1:37-39). In a certain sense, the spiritual life of the person who is preparing for the priesthood is dominated by this search: by it and by the "finding" of the Master, to follow him, to be in communion with him. So inexhaustible is the mystery of the imitation of Christ and the sharing in his life, that this "seeking" will also have to continue throughout the priest's life and ministry. Likewise this "finding" the Master will have to continue, in order to bring him to others, or rather in order to excite in others the desire to seek out the Master. But all this becomes possible if it is proposed to others as a living "experience", an experience that is worthwhile sharing. This was the path followed by Andrew to lead his brother Simon to Jesus. The Evangelist John writes that Andrew "first found his brother Simon, and said to him, 'We have found the Messiah' (which means Christ)" and brought him to Jesus (*Jn* 1:41-42). And so Simon too will be called, as an apostle, to follow the Messiah: "Jesus looked at him, and said, 'So you are Simon the son of John? You shall be called Cephas' (which means Peter)" (*Jn* 1:42).

But what does to seek Christ signify in the spiritual life? And, where is he to be found? "Rabbi, where are you staying?" The Decree *Optatam Totius* would seem to indicate a triple path to be covered: a faithful meditation on the word of God, active participation in the Church's holy mysteries and the service of charity to the "little ones". These are three great values and demands which further define the content of the spiritual formation of the candidate to the priesthood.

47.   An essential element of spiritual formation is *the prayerful and meditated reading of the word of God (lectio divina),* a humble and loving listening of him who speaks. It is in fact by the light and with the strength of the word of God that one's own vocation can be discovered and understood, loved and followed, and one's own mission carried out. So true is this that the person's entire existence finds its unifying and radical meaning in being the terminus of God's word which calls man and the beginning of man's word which answers God. Familiarity with the word of God will make conversion easy, not only in the sense of detaching us from evil so as to adhere to the good, but also in the sense of nourishing our heart with the thoughts of God, so that the faith (as a response to the word) becomes our new basis for judging and evaluating persons and things, events and problems.

Provided that we approach the word of God and listen to it as it really is, it brings us into contact with God himself, God speaking to man. It brings us into contact with Christ, the Word of God, the Truth who is at the same time both the Way and the Life (cf. *Jn* 14:6). It is a matter of reading the "scriptures" by listening to the "words", "the word" of God, as the Council reminds us: "The sacred scriptures contain the word of God and, because they are inspired, are truly the word of God".[138] The Council also states: "By this revelation, then, the invisible God (cf. *Col* 1:15; *1 Tim* 1:7), from the fullness of his love, addresses men as his friends (cf. *Ex* 33:11; *Jn* 15:14-15), and moves among them (cf. *Bar* 3:38), in order to invite and receive them into his own company".[139]

A loving knowledge of the word of God and a prayerful familiarity with it are specifically important for the prophetic ministry of the priest. They are a fundamental condition for such a ministry to be carried out suitably, especially if we bear in mind the "new evangelization" which the Church today is called to undertake. The Council tells us: "All clerics, particularly priests of Christ and others who, as deacons or catechists, are officially engaged in the ministry of the word, should immerse themselves in the Scriptures by constant sacred reading and diligent study. For it must not happen that anyone becomes 'an empty preacher of the word of God to others, not being a hearer of the word of God in his own heart' (ST AUGUSTINE, *Sermon* 179,1: *PL* 8:966)".[140]

The first and fundamental manner of responding to the word is *prayer*, which is without any doubt a primary value and demand of spiritual formation. Prayer should lead candidates for

---

[138] Dogmatic Constitution on Divine Revelation *Dei Verbum*, 24.
[139] *Ibid.*, 2.
[140] *Ibid.*, 25.

the priesthood to get to know and have experience of *the genuine meaning of Christian prayer,* as a living and personal meeting with the Father through the only-begotten Son under the action of the Spirit, a dialogue that becomes a sharing in the filial conversation between Jesus and the Father. One aspect of the priest's mission, and certainly by no means a secondary aspect, is that he is to be a "teacher of prayer". However, the priest will only be able to train others in this school of Jesus at prayer, if he himself has been trained in it and continues to receive its formation. This is what people ask of the priest: "The priest is *the man of God,* the one who belongs to God and makes people think about God. When the *Letter to the Hebrews* speaks of Christ it presents him as 'a merciful and faithful high priest in the service of God' (*Heb* 2:17)... Christians expect to find in the priest not only a man who welcomes them, who listens to them gladly and shows a real interest in them, but also and above all *a man who will help them to turn to God,* to rise up to him. And so the priest needs to be trained to have a deep intimacy with God. Those who are preparing for the priesthood should realize that their whole priestly life will have value inasmuch as they are able to give themselves to Christ and, through Christ, to the Father".[141]

A necessary training in prayer in a context of noise and agitation like that of our society,

---

[141] *Angelus* (4 March 1990), 2-3: *L'Osservatore Romano,* 5-6 March 1990.

is an education in the deep human meaning and religious value of *silence,* as the spiritual atmosphere vital for perceiving God's presence and for allowing oneself be won over by it (cf. *1 Kg* 19:11ff.).

48.   The high point of Christian prayer is the *Eucharist,* which in its turn is to be seen as the *"summit and source" of the sacraments and the Liturgy of the Hours.* A totally necessary aspect of the formation of every Christian, and in particular of every priest, is *liturgical formation,* in the full sense of becoming inserted in a living way in the Paschal Mystery of Jesus Christ who died and rose again, and is present and active in the Church's sacraments. Communion with God, which is the hinge on which the whole of the spiritual life turns, is the gift and fruit of the sacraments. At the same time it is a task and responsibility which the sacraments entrust to the freedom of the believer, so that he may live this same communion, in the decisions, choices, attitudes and actions of his daily existence. In this sense, the "grace" which "renews" Christian living is the grace of Jesus Christ who died and rose again, and continues to pour out his holy and sanctifying Spirit in the sacraments. In the same way, the "new law" which should guide and govern the life of the Christian is written by the sacraments in the "new heart". And it is a law of charity towards God and the brethren, as a response and prolonging of the charity of God towards man signified and communicated by the sacraments. It is

thus possible to understand straightaway the value of a "full, conscious and active participation"[142] in sacramental celebrations for the gift and task of that "pastoral charity" which is the soul of the priestly ministry.

This applies above all to sharing in the Eucharist, the memorial of the sacrificial death of Christ and of his glorious Resurrection, the "sacrament of piety, sign of unity, bond of charity",[143] the paschal banquet "in which Christ is received, the soul is filled with grace and we are given a pledge of the glory that is to be ours".[144] For priests, as ministers of sacred things, are first and foremost ministers of the Sacrifice of the Mass:[145] the role is utterly irreplaceable, because without the priest there can be no eucharistic offering.

This explains the essential importance of the Eucharist for the priest's life and ministry and, as a result, in the spiritual formation of candidates for the priesthood. To be utterly frank and clear, I would like to say once again: "It is fitting that seminarians take part *every day* in the eucharistic celebration, in such a way that afterwards they will take up as a rule of their priestly life this daily celebration. They should moreover be trained to consider the eucharistic celebration as the *essential moment of their day,* in which they will take an ac-

---

[142] SECOND VATICAN ECUMENICAL COUNCIL, Constitution on the Sacred Liturgy *Sacrosanctum Concilium,* 14.
[143] SAINT AUGUSTINE, *In Iohannis Evangelium Tractatus* 26,13: *loc. cit.,* 266.
[144] LITURGY OF THE HOURS, Magnificat Antiphon of Second Vespers of the Solemnity of the Body and Blood of Christ.
[145] Cf. SECOND VATICAN ECUMENICAL COUNCIL, Decree on the Ministry and Life of Priests *Presbyterorum Ordinis,* 13.

tive part and at which they will never be satisfied with a merely habitual attendance. Finally, candidates to the priesthood will be trained to share in the *intimate* dispositions which the Eucharist fosters: *gratitude* for heavenly benefits received, because the Eucharist is thanksgiving; *an attitude of self-offering* which will impel them to unite the offering of themselves to the eucharistic offering of Christ; *charity* nourished by a sacrament which is a sign of unity and sharing; *the yearning to contemplate and bow in adoration* before Christ who is really present under the eucharistic species".[146]

It is necessary and very urgent to rediscover, within spiritual formation, *the beauty and joy of the Sacrament of Penance*. In a culture which, through renewed and more subtle forms of self-justification, runs the fatal risk of losing the "sense of sin" and, as a result, the consoling joy of the plea for forgiveness (cf. *Ps* 51:14) and of meeting God who is "rich in mercy" (*Eph* 2:4), it is vital to educate future priests to have the virtue of penance, which the Church wisely nourishes in her celebrations and in the seasons of the liturgical year, and which finds its fullness in the sacrament of Reconciliation. From it flow the sense of asceticism and interior discipline, a spirit of sacrifice and self-denial, the acceptance of hard work and of the Cross. These are elements of the spiritual life which often prove to be particularly arduous for many candidates for the priesthood who have grown up in relatively comfortable and affluent

---

[146] *Angelus* (1 July 1990), 3: *L'Osservatore Romano,* 2-3 July 1990.

circumstances and have been made less inclined and open to these very elements by the models of behaviour and ideals transmitted by the mass media; but this also happens in countries where the conditions of life are poorer and young people live in more austere situations. For this reason, but above all in order to put into practice the "radical self-giving" proper to the priest following the example of Christ the Good Shepherd, the Synod Fathers wrote: "It is necessary to inculcate the meaning of the Cross, which is at the heart of the Paschal Mystery. Through this identification with Christ crucified, as a slave, the world can rediscover the value of austerity, of suffering and also of martyrdom, within the present culture which is imbued with secularism, greed and hedonism". [147]

49.   Spiritual formation also involves seeking Christ in people.

The spiritual life is, indeed, an interior life, a life of intimacy with God, a life of prayer and contemplation. But this very meeting with God, and with his fatherly love for everyone, brings us face to face with the need to meet our neighbour, to give ourselves to others, to serve in a humble and disinterested fashion, following the example which Jesus has proposed to everyone as a programme of life when he washed the feet of the apostles: "I have given you an example, that you also should do as I have done to you" (*Jn* 13:15).

[147] *Propositio* 23.

Formation which aims at giving oneself gener- ously and freely, which is something helped also by the communal structure which preparation to the priesthood normally takes, is a necessary con- dition for one who is called to be a manifestation and image of the Good Shepherd who gives life (cf. *Jn* 10:11, 15). From this point of view, spiri- tual formation has and should develop its own in- herent pastoral and charitable dimension, and can profitably make use of a proper devotion to the Sacred Heart of Jesus, one that is both strong and tender. This is a point made by the Synod Fathers: "When we speak of forming future priests in the spirituality of the Heart of the Lord, we mean they should lead lives that are a response to the love and affection of Christ the Priest and Good Shepherd: to his love for the Father in the Holy Spirit, and to his love towards men that was so great as to lead him to give his life in sacrifice for them".[148]

The priest is, therefore, a *man of charity,* and is called to educate others according to Christ's example and the new commandment of brotherly love (cf. *Jn* 15:12). But this demands that he him- self allow himself to be constantly trained by the Spirit in the charity of Christ. In this sense pre- paration for the priesthood must necessarily in- volve a proper training in charity and particularly in the preferential love for the "poor" in whom our faith discovers Jesus (cf. *Mt* 25:40), and a merciful love for sinners.

[148] *Ibid.*

In the general context of charity, which consists in the loving gift of oneself, is to be found, in the programme of spiritual formation of the future priest, *education in obedience, celibacy and poverty.*[149] The Council offers this invitation: "Students must clearly understand that it is not their lot in life to lord it over others and enjoy honours, but to devote themselves completely to the service of God and the pastoral ministry. With special care they should be trained in priestly obedience, poverty and a spirit of self-denial, that they may accustom themselves to living in conformity with the crucified Christ and to give up willingly even those things which are lawful, but not expedient".[150]

50.   The spiritual formation of one who is called to live celibacy should pay particular attention to preparing the future priest so that he may *know, appreciate, love and live celibacy according to its true nature* and according to its real purposes, that is for evangelical, spiritual and pastoral motives. The virtue of chastity is a premise for this preparation and is its content. It colours all human relations and leads "to experiencing and showing... a sincere, human, fraternal and personal love, one that is capable of sacrifice, following Christ's example, a love for all and for each person".[151]

---

[149] Cf. *ibid.*
[150] Decree on Priestly Formation *Optatam Totius,* 9.
[151] SACRED CONGREGATION FOR CATHOLIC EDUCATION, *Ratio Fundamentalis Institutionis Sacerdotalis* (6 January 1970), *loc. cit.,* 354.

The celibacy of priests brings with it certain characteristics, thanks to which they "renounce marriage for the sake of the kingdom of heaven (cf. Mt 19:12) and hold fast to their Lord with that undivided love which is profoundly in harmony with the New Covenant; they bear witness to the resurrection in a future life (cf. *Lk* 20:36) and obtain the most useful assistance towards the constant exercise of that perfect charity by which they can become all things to all men in their priestly ministry".[152] And so priestly celibacy should not be considered just as a legal norm, or as a totally external condition for admission to ordination, but rather as a value that is profoundly connected with ordination, whereby a man takes on the likeness of Jesus Christ, the good Shepherd and Spouse of the Church, and therefore as a choice of a greater and undivided love for Christ and his Church, as a full and joyful availability in his heart for the pastoral ministry. Celibacy is to be considered as a special grace, as a gift, for "not all men can receive this saying, but only those to whom it is given" (*Mt* 19:11). Certainly it is a grace which does not dispense with, but counts most definitely on, a conscious and free response on the part of the receiver. This charism of the Spirit also brings with it the grace for the receiver to remain faithful to it for all his life and be able to carry out generously and joyfully its concomitant commitments. Formation in priestly celibacy

---

[152] SECOND VATICAN ECUMENICAL COUNCIL, Decree on Priestly Formation *Optatam Totius,* 10.

137

should also include helping people to be aware of the "precious gift of God",[153] which will lead to prayer and to vigilance in guarding the gift from anything which could put it under threat.

Through his celibate life, the priest will be able to fulfil better his ministry on behalf of the People of God. In particular, as he witnesses to the evangelical value of virginity, he will be able to aid Christian spouses to live fully the "great sacrament" of the love of Christ the Bridegroom for his Spouse the Church, just as his own faithfulness to celibacy will help them to be faithful to each other as husband and wife.[154]

The importance of a careful preparation for priestly celibacy, especially in the social and cultural situations that we see today, led the Synod Fathers to make a series of requests which have a permanent value, as the wisdom of our Mother the Church confirms. I authoritatively set them down again as criteria to be followed in formation for chastity in celibacy: "Let the Bishops together with the rectors and spiritual directors of the seminaries establish principles, offer criteria and give assistance for discernment in this matter. Of the greatest importance for formation for chastity in celibacy are the Bishop's concern and fraternal life among priests. In the seminary, that is in the programme of formation, celibacy should be presented clearly, without any ambiguities and in a positive fashion. The seminarian should have a

---

[153] *Ibid.*
[154] *Letter to all the Priests of the Church on Holy Thursday 1979* (8 April 1979): *Insegnamenti* II/1 (1979), 841-862.

138

sufficient degree of psychological and sexual maturity as well as an assiduous and authentic life of prayer, and he should put himself under the direction of a spiritual father. The spiritual director should help the seminarian so that he himself reaches a mature and free decision, which is built on esteem for priestly friendship and self-discipline, as well as on the acceptance of solitude and on a physically and psychologically sound personal state. Therefore, seminarians should have a good knowledge of the teaching of the Second Vatican Council, of the Encyclical *Sacerdotalis Coelibatus* and the "Instruction for Formation in Priestly Celibacy" published by the Congregation for Catholic Education in 1974. In order that the seminarian may be able to embrace priestly celibacy for the Kingdom of Heaven with a free decision, he needs to know the Christian and truly human nature and purpose of sexuality in marriage and in celibacy. It is necessary also to instruct and educate the lay faithful regarding the evangelical, spiritual and pastoral reasons proper to priestly celibacy, so that they will help priests with their friendship, understanding and cooperation".[155]

INTELLECTUAL FORMATION: UNDERSTANDING THE FAITH

51.   Intellectual formation has its own characteristics but it is also deeply connected with, and indeed can be seen as a necessary expression of,

---

[155] *Propositio* 24.

both human and spiritual formation: it is a fundamental demand of man's intelligence by which he "participates in the light of God's mind" and seeks to acquire a wisdom which in turn opens to and is directed towards knowing and adhering to God.[156]

The intellectual formation of candidates for the priesthood finds its specific justification in the very nature of the ordained ministry, and the challenge of the "new evangelization" to which our Lord is calling the Church on the threshold of the third millennium shows just how important this formation is. "If we expect every Christian—the Synod Fathers write—to be prepared to make a defence of the faith and to account for the hope that is in us (cf. 1 Pt 3:15), then all the more should candidates for the priesthood and priests have diligent care of the quality of their intellectual formation in their education and pastoral activity. For the salvation of their brothers and sisters they should seek an ever deeper knowledge of the divine mysteries".[157] The present situation is heavily marked by religious indifference, by a widespread mistrust regarding the real capacity of reason to reach objective and universal truth, and by fresh problems and questions brought up by scientific and technological discoveries. It strongly demands a high level of intellectual formation, such as will enable priests to proclaim, in a context like this, the changeless Gospel of Christ and to

[156] SECOND VATICAN ECUMENICAL COUNCIL, Pastoral Constitution on the Church in the Modern World *Gaudium et Spes*, 15.
[157] *Propositio* 26.

make it credible to the legitimate demands of human reason. Moreover, there is the present phenomenon of pluralism which is very marked in the field not only of human society but also of the community of the Church herself. It demands special attention to critical discernment: it is a further reason showing the need for an extremely rigorous intellectual formation.

These "pastoral" reasons for intellectual formation reconfirm what has been said above concerning the unity of the educational process in its diverse aspects. The commitment to study, which takes up no small part of the time of those preparing for the priesthood, is not in fact an external and secondary dimension of their human, Christian, spiritual and vocational growth. In reality, through study, especially the study of theology, the future priest assents to the word of God, grows in his spiritual life and prepares himself to fulfil his pastoral ministry. This is the many-sided and unifying scope of the theological study indicated by the Council [158] and reproposed by the Synod's *Instrumentum Laboris:* "To be pastorally effective, intellectual formation is to be integrated with a spirituality marked by a personal experience of God. In this way a purely abstract approach to knowledge is overcome in favour of that intelligence of heart which knows how 'to look beyond', and then is in a position to communicate the mystery of God to the people". [159]

[158] Decree on Priestly Formation *Optatam Totius,* 16
[159] "The Formation of Priests in the Circumstances of the Present Day", *Instrumentum Laboris,* 39.

52.   A crucial stage of intellectual formation is
the study of *philosophy,* which leads to a deeper
understanding and interpretation of the person,
and of the person's freedom and relationships
with the world and with God. A proper philosophical training is vital, not only because of the
links between the great philosophical questions
and the mysteries of salvation which are studied in
theology under the guidance of the higher light of
faith,[160] but also vis-à-vis an extremely widespread
cultural situation which emphasizes subjectivism
as a criterion and measure of truth: only a sound
philosophy can help candidates for the priesthood
to develop a reflective awareness of the fundamental relationship that exists between the human
spirit and truth, that truth which is revealed to us
fully in Jesus Christ. Nor must one underestimate
the importance of philosophy as a guarantee of
that "certainty of truth" which is the only firm basis for a total giving of oneself to Jesus and to the
Church. It is not difficult to see that some very
specific questions, such as that concerning the
priest's identity and his apostolic and missionary
commitment, are closely linked to the question
about the nature of truth, which is anything but
an abstract question: if we are not certain about
the truth, how can we put our whole life on the
line, how can we have the strength to challenge
others' way of living?

Philosophy greatly helps the candidate to en-

---

[160] Cf. SACRED CONGREGATION FOR CATHOLIC EDUCATION,
Letter to Bishops *De necessitate Philosophiae studia in Seminariis impen-
sius promovendi* (20 January 1972).

142

rich his intellectual formation in the "cult of truth", namely, in a kind of *loving veneration of the truth,* which leads one to recognize that the truth is not created or measured by man but is given to man as a gift by the supreme Truth, God; that, albeit in a limited way and often with difficulty, human reason can reach objective and universal truth, even that relating to God and the radical meaning of existence; and that faith itself cannot do without reason and the effort of "thinking through" its contents, as that great mind Augustine bore witness: "I wished to see with my mind what I have believed, and I have argued and laboured greatly".[161]

For a deeper understanding of man and the phenomena and lines of development of society, in relation to a pastoral ministry which is as "incarnate" as possible, the so-called *"human sciences"* can be of considerable use, sciences such as sociology, psychology, education, economics and politics, and the science of social communication. Also in the precise field of the positive or descriptive sciences, these can help the future priest prolong the living "contemporaneousness" of Christ. As Paul VI once said, "Christ became the contemporary of some men and spoke their language. Our faithfulness to him demands that this contemporaneousness should be maintained".[162]

---

[161] *"Desideravi intellectu videre quod credidi, et multum disputavi et laboravi", De Trinitate* XV, 28: *CCL* 50/A, 534.

[162] PAUL VI, *Address to the participants in the 21st Italian Biblical Week* (25 September 1970): *AAS* 62 (1970), 618.

53. The intellectual formation of the future priest is based and built above all on the study of *sacred doctrine,* of theology. The value and genuineness of this theological formation depend on maintaining a scrupulous respect for the nature of theology. The Synod Fathers summarised this as follows: "True theology proceeds from the faith and aims at leading to the faith".[163] This is the conception of theology which has always been put forward by the Church and, specifically, by her Magisterium. This is the line followed by the great theologians who have enriched the Church's thinking down the ages. Saint Thomas is extremely clear when he affirms that the faith is as it were the *habitus* of theology, that is, its permanent principle of operation,[164] and that the whole of theology is ordered to nourishing the faith.[165]

The theologian is therefore, first and foremost, a believer, a man of faith. But he is a believer who asks himself questions about his own faith (*fides quaerens intellectum*), with the aim of reaching a deeper understanding of the faith itself. The two aspects (of faith and mature reflection) are intimately connected, intertwined: their intimate coordination and interpenetration are what makes for true theology, and as a result decide the contents, modalities and spirit according to which the sacred doctrine (*sacra doctrina*) is elaborated and studied.

[163] *Propositio* 26.
[164] *"Fides, quae est quasi habitus theologiae"*: In *Lib. Boethii de Trinitate,* V,4 ad 8.
[165] "Cf. Saint Thomas, *In I Sentent.,* Prolog., q. I, a. 1-5.

Moreover, since the faith, which is the point of departure and the point of arrival of theology, brings about a personal relationship between the believer and Jesus Christ in the Church, theology also has intrinsic Christological and ecclesial connotations, which the candidate to the priesthood should take up consciously, not only because of what they imply for his personal life but also inasmuch as they affect his pastoral ministry. If our faith truly welcomes the word of God, it will lead to a radical "yes" on the part of the believer to Jesus Christ, who is the full and definitive Word of God to the world (cf. *Heb* 1:1ff.). As a result, theological reflection is centred on adherence to Jesus Christ, the Wisdom of God: mature reflection has to be described as a sharing in the "thinking" of Christ (cf. *1 Cor* 2:16) in the human form of a science (*scientia fidei*). At the same time, faith inserts the believer in the Church and makes him partake in the life of the Church as a community of faith. Hence theology has an ecclesial dimension, because it is a mature reflection on the faith of the Church by the theologian who is a member of the Church.[166]

These Christological and ecclesial dimensions which are connatural to theology, while they help candidates for the priesthood grow in scientific precision, will also help them develop a great and living love for Jesus Christ and for his Church. This love will both nourish their spiritual life and guide them to carry out their ministry with a gen-

---

[166] Cf. CONGREGATION FOR THE DOCTRINE OF THE FAITH, Instruction on the Ecclesial Vocation of the Theologian *Donum Veritatis* (24 May 1990), 11; 40: *AAS* 82 (1990), 1554-1555; 1568-1569.

erous spirit. This was what the Second Vatican Council had in mind when it called for a revision of ecclesiastical studies, with a view to "a more effective coordination of philosophy and theology so that they supplement one another in revealing to the minds of the students with ever increasing clarity the Mystery of Christ, which affects the whole course of human history, exercises an unceasing influence on the Church, and operates mainly through the ministry of the priest".[167]

Intellectual formation in theology and formation in the spiritual life, in particular the life of prayer, meet and strengthen each other, without detracting in any way from the soundness of research or from the spiritual tenor of prayer. Saint Bonaventure reminds us: "Let no one think that it is enough for him to read if he lacks devotion, or to engage in speculation without spiritual joy, or to be active if he has no piety, or to have knowledge without charity, or intelligence without humility, or study without God's grace, or to expect to know himself if he is lacking the infused wisdom of God".[168]

54.   Theological formation is both complex and demanding. It should lead the candidate for the priesthood to *a complete and unified vision* of the truths which God has revealed in Jesus Christ and of the Church's experience of faith. Hence the need both to know "all" the Christian truths,

---

[167] Decree on Priestly Formation *Optatam Totius*, 14.
[168] *Itinerarium mentis in Deum,* Prol., 4: *Opera Omnia,* Tomus V, Ad Aquas Claras 1891, 296.

without arbitrarily selecting among them, and to know them in an orderly fashion. This means the candidate needs to be helped to build a synthesis which will be the result of the contributions of the different theological disciplines, the specific nature of which acquires genuine value only in their profound coordination.

In reflecting maturely upon the faith, theology moves in two directions. The first is that of the *study of the word of God:* the word set down in Holy Writ, celebrated and lived in the living Tradition of the Church, and authoritatively interpreted by the Church's Magisterium. Hence the importance of studying Sacred Scripture—"which should be the soul, as it were, of all theology",[169] the Fathers of the Church, the liturgy, the history of the Church and the teachings of the Magisterium. The second direction is that of *man, who converses with God:* man who is called "to believe", "to live", "to communicate" to others the *Christian faith* and *outlook.* Hence the study of dogmatic and moral theology, of spiritual theology, of canon law and of pastoral theology.

Because of its relationship to the believer theology is led to pay particular attention both to the fundamental and permanent question of the relationship between faith and reason and to a number of requirements more closely related to the social and cultural situation of today. In regard to the first we have the study of fundamental

---

[169] SECOND VATICAN ECUMENICAL COUNCIL, Decree on Priestly Formation *Optatam Totius,* 16.

theology, whose object is the fact of Christian revelation and its transmission in the Church. In regard to the second we have disciplines which have been and are being developed as responses to problems strongly felt nowadays. This is true of the study of the Church's social doctrine which "belongs to the field... of theology and, in particular, of moral theology" [170] and is to be counted among the "essential components" of the "new evangelization", of which it is an instrument. [171] This is likewise true of the study of missiology, ecumenism, Judaism, Islam and other religions.

55. Theological formation nowadays should pay attention to *certain problems* which not infrequently raise difficulties, tensions and confusion within the life of the Church. One can think of the *relationship between statements issued by the Magisterium and theological discussion,* a relationship which does not always take the shape it ought to have, that is, within a framework of cooperation. It is indeed true that "the living Magisterium of the Church and theology, while having different gifts and functions, ultimately have the same goal: preserving the People of God in the truth which sets free and thereby making them 'a light to the nations'. This service to the ecclesial community brings the theologian and the Magisterium

---

[170] Encyclical Letter *Sollicitudo Rei Socialis* (30 December 1987), 41: *AAS* 80 (1988), 571.
[171] Cf. Encyclical Letter *Centesimus Annus* (1 May 1991), 54: *AAS* 83 (1991), 859-860.

into a mutual relationship. The latter authentically teaches the doctrine of the Apostles. And, benefitting from the work of theologians, it refutes objections to and distortions of the faith, and promotes, with the authority received from Jesus Christ, new and deeper comprehension, clarification, and application of revealed doctrine. Theology, for its part, gains, by way of reflection, an ever deeper understanding of the word of God found in the Scripture and handed on faithfully by the Church's living Tradition under the guidance of the Magisterium. Theology strives to clarify the teaching of Revelation with regard to reason and gives it finally an organic and systematic form". [172] When, for a number of reasons, this cooperation is lacking, one needs to avoid misunderstandings and confusion, and to know how to distinguish carefully "the common teaching of the Church from the opinions of theologians and from tendencies which quickly pass (the so-called 'trends')". [173] There is no "parallel" magisterium, for the one Magisterium is that of Peter and the Apostles, the Pope and the Bishops. [174]

Another problem, which is experienced especially when seminary studies are entrusted to

---

[172] CONGREGATION FOR THE DOCTRINE OF THE FAITH, Instruction on the Ecclesial Vocation of the Theologian *Donum Veritatis* (24 May 1990), 21: *loc. cit.,* 1559.

[173] *Propositio* 26.

[174] For example, Saint Thomas Aquinas wrote: "We have to be more on the side of the authority of the Church than on that of Augustine or Jerome, or any other Doctor" (*Summa Theol.* II-II, q. 10, a. 12). And again: "No one can shield himself with the authority of Jerome or Augustine or any other Doctor against the authority of Peter" (*ibid.,* I-II, q. 11, a. 2 ad 3).

149

academic institutions, is that of the *relationship between high scientific standards in theology and its pastoral aim.* This raises the issue of the pastoral nature of theology. It is a question, really, of two characteristics of theology and how it is to be taught which are not only not opposed to each other, but which work together, from different angles, in favour of a more complete "understanding of the faith". In fact the pastoral nature of theology does not mean that it should be less doctrinal or that it should be completely stripped of its scientific nature. It means, rather, that it enables future priests to proclaim the Gospel message through the cultural modes of their age and to direct pastoral action according to an authentic theological vision. Hence, on the one hand, a respectful study of the genuine scientific quality of the individual disciplines of theology will help provide a more complete and deeper training of the pastor of souls as a teacher of faith. And, on the other hand, an appropriate awareness that there is a pastoral goal in view will help the serious and scientific study of theology be more formative for future priests.

A further problem that is strongly felt these days is the demand for the *evangelization of cultures* and the *inculturation of the message of faith.* An eminently pastoral problem, this should enter more broadly and carefully into the formation of the candidates to the priesthood: "In the present circumstances in which, in a number of regions of the world, the Christian religion is considered as something foreign to cultures (be they ancient or modern), it is very important that in the whole intellectual and human formation the dimension of inculturation be seen as necessary and essential".[175] But this means we need a genuine theology, inspired by the Catholic principles on inculturation. These principles are linked with the mystery of the incarnation of the Word of God and with Christian anthropology and thus illumine the authentic meaning of inculturation. In the face of all the different and at times contrasting cultures present in the various parts of the world, inculturation seeks to obey Christ's command to preach the Gospel to all nations even unto the ends of the earth. Such obedience does not signify either syncretism or a simple adaptation of the announcement of the Gospel, but rather the fact that the Gospel penetrates the very life of cultures, becomes incarnate in them, overcoming those cultural elements that are incompatible with the faith and Christian living and raising their values to the mystery of salvation which comes from Christ.[176] The problem of inculturation can have a particularly great interest when the candidates to the priesthood are themselves coming from indigenous cultures. In that case, they will need to find suitable ways of formation, both to overcome the danger of being less demanding and to

[175] Propositio 32.
[176] Cf. Encyclical Letter Redemptoris Missio (7 December 1990), 67: loc. cit., 315-316.

151

proper use of the good and genuine elements of their own cultures and traditions.[177]

56.   Following the teaching and the indications of the Second Vatican Council and their application in the *Ratio Fundamentalis Institutionis Sacerdotalis,* the Church decided upon a vast updating of the teaching of the philosophical and especially theological disciplines in seminaries. This updating, which in some cases still needs amendments and developments, has on the whole helped to make the education available a more effective medium for intellectual formation. In this respect "the Synod Fathers have confirmed once again, frequently and clearly, the need—indeed the urgency—to put the basic study plan (both the general one which applies to the Church worldwide, and those of the individual nations or Episcopal Conferences) into effect in seminaries and in houses of formation".[178]

It is necessary to oppose firmly the tendency to play down the seriousness of studies and the commitment to them. This tendency is showing itself in certain spheres of the Church, also as a consequence of the insufficient and defective basic education of students beginning the philosophical and theological curriculum. The very situation of the Church today demands increasingly that teachers be truly able to face the complexity of the times and that they be in a position to face com-

---

[177] Cf. *Propositio* 32.
[178] *Propositio* 27.

petently, with clarity and deep reasoning, the questions about meaning which are put by the people of today, questions which can only receive a full and definitive reply in the Gospel of Jesus Christ.

PASTORAL FORMATION: COMMUNION WITH THE CHARITY OF JESUS CHRIST THE GOOD SHEPHERD

57. The whole formation imparted to candidates for the priesthood aims at preparing them to enter into communion with the charity of Christ the Good Shepherd. Hence, their formation in its different aspects must have a fundamentally pastoral character. The Council's Decree *Optatam Totius* states so clearly when speaking of Major Seminaries: "The whole training of the students should have as its object to make them *true shepherds of souls after the example of our Lord Jesus Christ, teacher, priest and shepherd.* Hence, they should be trained for the ministry of the word so that they may gain an ever increasing understanding of the revealed word of God, making it their own by meditation, and giving it expression in their speech and in their lives. They should be trained for the ministry of worship and sanctification, so that by prayer and the celebration of the sacred liturgical functions they may carry on the work of salvation through the eucharistic sacrifice and the sacraments. They should be trained to undertake the ministry of the shepherd, that they may know how to represent Christ to humanity,

Christ who 'did not come to have service done to him but to serve others and to give his life as a ransom for the lives of many' (*Mk* 10:45; *Jn* 13:12-17), and that they may win over many by becoming the servants of all (*1 Cor* 9:19)".[179]

The Council text insists upon the coordination of the different aspects of human, spiritual, and intellectual formation. At the same time it stresses that they are all directed to a specific pastoral end. This pastoral aim ensures that the human, spiritual and intellectual formation has certain precise content and characteristics; it also unifies and gives specificity to the whole formation of future priests.

Like all other branches of formation, pastoral formation develops by means of mature reflection and practical application, and it is rooted in a spirit, which is the hinge of all and the force which stimulates it and makes it develop.

It needs to be studied therefore as the true and genuine theological discipline that it is: *pastoral or practical theology*. It is a scientific reflection on the Church as she is built up daily, by the power of the Spirit, in history; on the Church as the "universal sacrament of salvation",[180] as a living sign and instrument of the salvation wrought by Christ through the word, the sacraments and the service of charity. Pastoral theology is not just an art. Nor is it a set of exhortations, experiences and methods. It is theological in its own right, be-

[179] Decree on Priestly Formation *Optatam Totius,* 4.
[180] SECOND VATICAN ECUMENICAL COUNCIL, Dogmatic Constitution on the Church *Lumen Gentium,* 48.

cause it receives from the faith the principles and criteria for the pastoral action of the Church in history, a Church that each day "begets" the Church herself, to quote the felicitous expression of the Venerable Bede: *"Nam et Ecclesia quotidie gignit Ecclesiam"*.[181] Among these principles and criteria one that is specially important is that of the evangelical discernment of the socio-cultural and ecclesial situation in which the particular pastoral action has to be carried out.

The study of pastoral theology should throw light upon its *practical application* through involvement in certain pastoral services which the candidates to the priesthood should carry out, with a necessary progression and always in harmony with their other educational commitments. It is a question of pastoral "experiences", which can come together in a real programme of "pastoral training", which can last a considerable amount of time and the usefulness of which will itself need to be checked in an orderly manner.

Pastoral study and action direct one to an inner source, which the work of formation will take care to guard and make good use of: this is the *ever deeper communion with the pastoral charity of Jesus,* which, just as it was the principle and driving force of his salvific action, likewise, thanks to the outpouring of the Holy Spirit in the Sacrament of Orders, should constitute the principle and driving force of the priestly ministry. It is a question of a type of formation meant not only to

---

[181] *Explanatio Apocalypsis,* lib. II, 12: *PL* 93,166.

ensure scientific, pastoral competence and practical skill, but also and especially a *way of being* in communion with the very sentiments and behaviour of Christ the Good Shepherd: "Have this mind among yourselves, which is yours in Christ Jesus" (*Phil* 2:5).

58.   And so pastoral formation certainly cannot be reduced to a mere apprenticeship, aiming to make the candidate familiar with some pastoral techniques. The seminary which educates must seek really and truly to initiate the candidate into the sensitivity of being a shepherd, in the conscious and mature assumption of his responsibilities, in the interior habit of evaluating problems and establishing priorities and looking for solutions on the basis of honest motivations of faith and according to the theological demands inherent in pastoral work.

   Thanks to an initial and gradual experience of ministry, future priests will be able to be inserted into the living pastoral tradition of their particular Church. They will learn to open the horizon of their mind and heart to the missionary dimension of the Church's life. They will get practice in some initial forms of cooperation with one another and with the priests alongside whom they will be sent to work. These priests have a considerably important role, in union with the seminary programme, in showing the candidates how they should go about pastoral work.

   When it comes to choosing places and services in which candidates can obtain their pastoral experience, the parish should be given particular importance,[182] for it is a living cell of local and specialized pastoral work, in which they will find themselves faced with the kind of problems they will meet in their future ministry. The Synod Fathers have proposed a number of concrete examples, such as visits to the sick; caring for immigrants, refugees and nomads; and various social works which can be expressions of charitable zeal. Specifically, they write: "The priest must be a witness of the charity of Christ himself who 'went about doing good' (*Acts* 10:38). He must also be a visible sign of the solicitude of the Church who is Mother and Teacher. And given that man today is affected by so many hardships, especially those who are sunk in inhuman poverty, blind violence and unjust power, it is necessary that the man of God who is to be equipped for every good work (cf. *2 Tim* 3:17), should defend the rights and dignity of man. Nevertheless, he should be careful not to adopt false ideologies, nor should he forget, as he strives to promote its perfecting, that the only redemption of the world is that effected by the Cross of Christ".[183]

These and other pastoral activities will teach the future priest to live out as a "service" his own mission of "authority" in the community, setting aside all attitudes of superiority or of exercising a power if it is not simply that which is justified by pastoral charity.

---

[182] Cf. *Propositio* 28.
[183] *Ibid.*

If the training is to be suitable, the different experiences which candidates for the priesthood have should assume a clear "ministerial" character, and should be intimately linked with all the demands that befit preparation to the priesthood and (certainly not neglecting their studies) in relation to the services of the proclamation of the word, of worship and of leadership. These services can become a specific way of experiencing the ministries of Lector, Acolyte and Deacon.

59.　Since pastoral action is destined by its very nature to enliven the Church, which is essentially "mystery", "communion" and "mission", pastoral formation should be aware of and should live these ecclesial aspects in the exercise of the ministry.

Of fundamental importance is awareness that the Church is a "mystery", that is, a divine work, fruit of the Spirit of Christ, an effective sign of grace, the presence of the Trinity in the Christian community. This awareness, while never lessening the pastor's genuine sense of responsibility, will convince him that the Church grows thanks to the gratuitous work of the Spirit and that his service—thanks to the very grace of God that is entrusted to the free responsibility of man—is the Gospel service of the "unworthy servant" (cf. *Lk* 17:10).

Awareness of the *Church* as *"communion"* will prepare the candidate for the priesthood to carry out his pastoral work with a community spirit, in heartfelt cooperation with the different members of the Church: priests and Bishop, diocesan and religious priests, priests and lay people. Such a co-operation presupposes a knowledge and appreciation of the different gifts and charisms, of the diverse vocations and responsibilities which the Spirit offers and entrusts to the members of Christ's Body. It demands a living and precise consciousness of one's own identity in the Church and of the identity of others. It demands mutual trust, patience, gentleness and the capacity for understanding and expectation. It finds it roots above all in a love for the Church that is deeper than love for self and the group or groups one may belong to. It is particularly important to prepare future priests for *cooperation with the laity.* The Council says, "they should be willing to listen to lay people, give brotherly consideration to their wishes and recognize their experience and competence in the different fields of human activity. In this way they will be able to recognize with them the signs of the times".[184] The recent Synod too has insisted upon pastoral solicitude for the laity: "The student should become capable of proposing and introducing the lay faithful, the young especially, to the different vocations (marriage, social services, apostolate, ministries and other responsibilities in pastoral activity, the consecrated life, involvement in political and social leadership, scientific research, teaching). Above all it is necessary that he be able to teach and support the laity in

---

[184] Decree on the Ministry and Life of Priests *Presbyterorum Ordinis*, 9; cf. Apostolic Exhortation *Christifideles Laici* (30 December 1981), 61: *loc. cit.*, 512-514.

their vocation to be present in and to transform the world with the light of the Gospel, by recognizing this task of theirs and showing respect for it".[185]

Lastly, awareness of the Church as a *"missionary" communion* will help the candidate for the priesthood to love and live the essential missionary dimension of the Church and her different pastoral activities. He should be open and available to all the possibilities offered today for the proclamation of the Gospel, not forgetting the valuable service which can and should be given by the media.[186] He should prepare himself for a ministry which may mean in practice that his readiness to follow the indications of the Holy Spirit and of his Bishop will lead him to be sent to preach the Gospel even beyond the frontiers of his own country.[187]

II. THE SETTING OF PRIESTLY FORMATION

The Major Seminary—a formation community

60.   *The need* for the Major Seminary—and by analogy for the Religious House—for the formation of candidates for the priesthood, was affirmed with authority by the Second Vatican Council [188] and has been *reaffirmed by the Synod* as

---

[185] *Propositio* 28.
[186] Cf. *ibid.*
[187] Cf. Encyclical Letter *Redemptoris Missio* (7 December 1990), 67-68: *loc. cit.,* 315-316.
[188] Cf. Decree on Priestly Formation *Optatam Totius,* 4.

follows: "The institution of the Major Seminary, as the best place for formation, is to be certainly reaffirmed as the normal place, in the material sense as well, for a community and hierarchical life, indeed as the proper home for the formation of candidates for the priesthood, with superiors who are truly dedicated to this service. This institution has produced many good results down the ages and continues to do so all over the world".[189]

The seminary can be seen as a place and a period in life. But it is above all an *educational community in progress:* it is a community established by the Bishop to offer to those called by the Lord to serve as Apostles the possibility of re-living the experience of formation which our Lord provided for the Twelve. In fact, the Gospels present a prolonged and intimate sharing of life with Jesus as a necessary premise for the apostolic ministry. Such an experience demands of the Twelve the practice of detachment in a particularly clear and specific fashion, a detachment that in some way is demanded of all the disciples, a detachment from their roots, from their usual work, from their nearest and dearest (cf. *Mk* 1:16-20; 10: 28; *Lk* 9:23, 57-62; 14:25-27). On several occasions we have referred to the Marcan tradition which stresses the deep link that unites the Apostles to Christ and to one another: before being sent out to preach and to heal, they are called "to be with him" (*Mk* 3:14).

In its deepest identity the seminary is called to

[189] *Propositio* 20.

be, in its own way, a *continuation in the Church of the apostolic community gathered about Jesus,* listening to his word, proceeding towards the Easter experience, awaiting the gift of the Spirit for the mission. Such an identity constitutes the normative ideal which stimulates the seminary, in the many diverse forms and varied aspects which it assumes historically as a *human institution,* to find a concrete realization, faithful to the gospel values from which it takes its inspiration, and able to respond to the situations and needs of the times.

The seminary is, in itself, *an original experience of the Church's life.* In it the Bishop is present through the ministry of the rector and the service of co-responsibility and communion fostered by him with the other teachers, for the sake of the pastoral and apostolic growth of the students. The various members of the seminary community, gathered by the Spirit into a single brotherhood, cooperate, each according to his own gift, in the growth of all in faith and charity, so that they may prepare suitably for the priesthood and so prolong in the Church and in history the saving presence of Jesus Christ, the Good Shepherd.

From the human point of view, the Major Seminary should strive to become "a community built on deep friendship and charity, so that it can be considered a true family living in joy".[190] As a Christian institution, the Seminary should become—as the Synod Fathers continue—an "ecclesial community", a "community of the disciples

[190] *Ibid.*

of the Lord in which the one same Liturgy (which imbues life with a spirit of prayer) is celebrated, a community moulded daily in the reading and meditation of the word of God and with the Sacrament of the Eucharist and in the practice of fraternal charity and justice, a community in which, as its life and the life of each of its members progresses, there shine forth the Spirit of Christ and love for the Church".[191] This ecclesial aspect of the Seminary is confirmed and concretized by the Fathers when they add: "As an ecclesial community, be it diocesan or interdiocesan, or even religious, the Seminary should nourish the meaning of communion between the candidates and their Bishop and Presbyterate, in such a way that they share in their hopes and anxieties and learn to extend this openness to the needs of the universal Church".[192]

It is essential for the formation of candidates for the priesthood and the pastoral ministry, which by its very nature is ecclesial, that the Seminary should be experienced not as something external and superficial, or simply a place in which to live and study, but in an interior and profound way. It should be experienced as a community, a specifically ecclesial community, a community that re-lives the experience of the group of Twelve who were united to Jesus.[193]

[191] Ibid.
[192] Ibid.
[193] Cf. Address to the students and former students of the Almo Collegio Capranica (21 January 1983): Insegnamenti VI/1 (1983), 173-178.

163

61.   The Seminary is, therefore, an *educational ecclesial community,* indeed a particular educating community. And it is the specific goal which determines its physiognomy: the vocational accompanying of future priests, and therefore discernment of a vocation, the help to respond to it and the preparation to receive the Sacrament of Orders with its own graces and responsibilities, by which the priest is configured to Jesus Christ Head and Shepherd and is enabled and committed to share the mission of salvation in the Church and in the world.

Inasmuch as it is an educating community, the Seminary and its entire life, in all its different expressions, is *committed to formation,* the human, spiritual, intellectual and pastoral formation of future priests. Although this formation has many aspects in common with the human and Christian formation of all the members of the Church, it has, nevertheless, contents, modalities and characteristics which relate specifically to the aim of preparation for the priesthood.

The content and form of the educational work require that the Seminary should have a precise *programme,* a programme of life characterized by its being organized and unified, by its being in harmony or correspondence with one aim which justifies the existence of the Seminary: preparation of future priests.

In this regard, the Synod Fathers write: "As an educational community, (the Seminary) should follow a clearly defined programme which will have, as a characteristic, a unity of leadership ex-

pressed in the figure of the Rector and his cooperators, a consistency in the ordering of life, formational activity and the fundamental demands of
community life, which also involves the essential
aspects of the task of formation. This programme
should be at the service of the specific finality
which alone justifies the existence of the Seminary
and it should do so without hesitation or ambiguity. That aim is the formation of future priests,
pastors of the Church".[194] And in order to ensure
that the programming is truly apt and effective,
the fundamental outlines of the programme will
have to be translated into more concrete details,
with the help of particular norms that are aimed at
regulating community life, establishing certain
precise instruments and timetables.

A further aspect is to be stressed here: the
educational work is by its nature an accompanying
of specific individual persons who are proceeding
to a choice of and commitment to precise ideals of
life. For this very reason, the work of education
should be able to bring together into an harmonious whole a clear statement of the goal to be
achieved, the requirement that candidates proceed
seriously towards the goal, and thirdly attention to
the "journeyer", that is the individual person who
is embarked on this adventure, and therefore attention to a series of situations, problems, difficulties, and different rates of progress and growth.
This requires a wise flexibility. And this does not
mean compromising, either as regards values or as

[194] *Propositio* 20.

regards the conscious and free commitment of the candidates. What it does mean is a true love and a sincere respect for the person who, in conditions which are very personal, is proceeding towards the priesthood. This applies not only to individual candidates, but also to the diverse social and cultural contexts in which seminaries exist and to the different life histories which they have. In this sense *the educational work requires continual renewal.* The Synod Fathers have brought this out forcefully also when speaking about the structure of Seminaries: "Without questioning the validity of the classical forms of Seminaries, the Synod desires that the work of consultation of the Episcopal Conferences on the present day needs of formation should proceed as is established in the Decree *Optatam Totius,* (No. 1) and in the 1967 Synod. The *Rationes* of the different nations or rites should be revised where opportune, whether on the occasion of requests made by the Episcopal Conferences or in relation to Apostolic Visitations of the Seminaries of different countries, in order to bring into them diverse forms of formation that have proved successful, as well as to respond to the needs of people with so-called indigenous cultures, the needs of the vocations of adult men, and the needs of vocations for the missions, etc.".[195]

62.   The purpose and specific educational form of the Major Seminary demand that candidates

[195] *Ibid.*

for the priesthood have *a certain prior preparation* before entering it. Such preparation, at least until a few decades ago, did not create particular problems. In those days most candidates to the priesthood came from Minor Seminaries, and the Christian life of the community offered all, in general, a suitable Christian instruction and education.

The situation in many places has changed. There is a considerable discrepancy between, on the one hand, the style of life and basic preparation of boys, adolescents and young men, even when they are Christians and at times have been involved in Church life, and, on the other hand, the style of life of the Seminary with its formational demands.

In this context, together with the Synod Fathers I ask that there be a sufficient period of preparation prior to Seminary formation: "It is a good thing that there be a period of human, Christian, intellectual and spiritual preparation for the candidates to the Major Seminary. These candidates should, however, have certain qualities: a right intention, a sufficient degree of human maturity, a sufficiently broad knowledge of the doctrine of the faith, some introduction into the methods of prayer, and behaviour in conformity with Christian tradition. They should also have attitudes proper to their regions, through which they can express their effort to find God and the faith (cf. *Evangelii Nuntiandi,* No. 48)".[196]

[196] *Propositio* 19.

The "sufficiently broad knowledge of the doctrine of the faith" which the Synod Fathers mention is a primary condition for theology. It simply is not possible to develop an *"intelligentia fidei"* (an understanding of the faith), if the content of the *"fides"* is not known. Such a gap can be filled more easily when the forthcoming *Universal Catechism* appears.

While there is increasing consensus regarding the need for preparation prior to the Major Seminary, there are different ideas as to what such preparation should contain and what its characteristics should be: should it be directed mainly to spiritual formation to discern the vocation or to intellectual and cultural formation? On the other hand, we cannot overlook the many and deep diversities that exist, not only among the individual candidates, but also in the different regions and countries. This implies the need for a period of study and experimentation in order to define as clearly and suitably as possible the different elements of this prior preparation or *"propaedeutic period"*: the duration, place, form, subject matter of this period, all of which will have to be coordinated with the subsequent years of formation offered by the Seminary.

In this sense I take up and propose to the Congregation for Catholic Education a request expressed by the Synod Fathers: "The Synod asks that the Congregation for Catholic Education gather all the information on experiments of such initial formation that have been done or are being done. At a suitable time, the Congregation is requested to communicate its findings on this matter to the Episcopal Conferences".[197]

The Minor Seminary and other forms of fostering vocations

63.   As long experience shows, a priestly vocation tends to show itself in the pre-adolescent years or in the earliest years of youth. Even in people who decide to enter the seminary later on it is not infrequent to find that God's call had been perceived much earlier. The Church's history gives constant witness of calls which the Lord directs to people of tender age. Saint Thomas, for example, explains Jesus' special love for Saint John the Apostle "because of his tender age" and draws the following conclusion: "This explains that God loves in a special way those who give themselves to his service from their earliest youth".[198]

The Church looks after these seeds of vocations sown in the hearts of children, by means of the institution of Minor Seminaries, providing a careful though preliminary discernment and accompaniment. In a number of parts of the world, these Seminaries continue to carry out a valuable educational work, the aim of which is to protect and develop the seeds of a priestly vocation, so that the students may more easily recognize it and be in a better position to respond to it. The edu-

[197] Ibid.
[198] In Iohannem Evangelistam Expositio, c. 21, lect. V, 2.

169

cational goal of such Seminaries tends to favour in a timely and gradual way the human, cultural and spiritual formation which will lead the young person to embark on the path of the Major Seminary with an adequate and solid foundation. *"To be prepared to follow Christ the Redeemer with generous souls and pure hearts":* this is the purpose of the Minor Seminary as indicated by the Council in the Decree *Optatam Totius,* which thus outlines its educational aspect: the students "under the fatherly supervision of the superiors, the parents too playing their appropriate part, should lead lives suited to the age, mentality and development of young people. Their way of life should be fully in keeping with the standards of sound psychology and should include suitable experience of the ordinary affairs of daily life and contact with their own families".[199]

The Minor Seminary can also be in the Diocese a reference point for vocation work, with suitable forms of welcome and the offering of opportunities for information to adolescents who are looking into the possibility of a vocation or who, having already made up their mind to follow their vocation, have to delay entry into the Seminary for various family or educational reasons.

64.   In those cases where it is not possible to run Minor Seminaries (which "in many regions seem necessary and very useful"), other "institutions" need to be provided, as for example *voca-*

---

[199] Decree on Priestly Formation *Optatam Totius,* 3.

tional groups for adolescents and young people.[200] While they lack the quality of permanence, such groups can offer a systematic guide, in a community context, with which to check the existence and development of vocations. While such young people live at home and take part in the activities of the Christian community which helps them along the path of formation, they should not be left alone. They need a particular group or community to refer to, and where they can find support to follow through the specific vocational journey which the gift of the Holy Spirit has initiated in them.

We should also mention the phenomenon of *priestly vocations* arising among people *of adult age,* after some years of experience of lay life and professional involvement. This phenomenon, while not new in the Church's history, at present appears with some novel features and with a certain frequency. It is not always possible and often it is not even convenient to invite adults to follow the educative itinerary of the Major Seminary. Rather, after a careful discernment of the genuineness of such vocations, what needs to be provided is some kind of specific programme to accompany them with formation in order to ensure, bearing in mind all the suitable adaptations, that such persons receive the spiritual and intellectual formation they require. A suitable relationship with other candidates to the priesthood and periods spent in the community of the Major

---

[200] Cf. *Propositio* 17.

Seminary can be a way of guaranteeing that these vocations are fully inserted in the one presbyterate and are in intimate and heartfelt communion with it.[201]

III. THE AGENTS OF PRIESTLY FORMATION

The Church and the Bishop

65.   Given that the formation of candidates for the priesthood belongs to the Church's pastoral care of vocations, it must be said that *the Church as such is the communal subject* which has the grace and responsibility to accompany those whom the Lord calls to becomes his ministers in the priesthood.

In this sense the appreciation of the mystery of the Church helps us to establish more precisely the place and role which her different members have—be it individually or as members of a body—in the formation of candidates for the priesthood.

The Church is by her very nature the "memorial" or "sacrament" of the presence and action of Jesus Christ in our midst and on our behalf. The call to the priesthood depends on his saving presence: not only the call, but also the accompanying so that the person called can recognize the Lord's grace and respond to it freely and lovingly.

---

[201] Cf. SACRED CONGREGATION FOR CATHOLIC EDUCATION, *Ratio Fundamentalis Institutionis Sacerdotalis* (6 January 1970), 19: *loc. cit.,* 342.

It is the Spirit of Jesus that throws light on and gives strength to vocational discernment and the journey to the priesthood. So we can say that *there cannot exist any genuine formational work for the priesthood without the influence of the Spirit of Christ.* Every one involved in the work of formation should be fully aware of this. How can we fail to appreciate this utterly gratuitous and completely effective "resource", which has its own decisive "weight" in the effort to train people for the priesthood? How can we not rejoice when we consider the dignity of every human being involved in formation, who for the candidate to the priesthood becomes, as it were, the visible representative of Christ? If training for the priesthood is, as it should be, essentially the preparation of future "shepherds" in the likeness of Jesus Christ the Good Shepherd, who better than Jesus himself, through the outpouring of his Spirit, can give them and fully develop in them that pastoral charity which he himself lived to the point of total self-giving (cf. *Jn* 15:13; 10:11) and which he wishes all priests to live in their turn?

The first representative of Christ in priestly formation is the Bishop. What Mark the Evangelist tells us, in the text we have already quoted more than once, can be applied to the Bishop, to every Bishop: "He called to him those whom he desired; and *they came to him.* And he appointed twelve *to be with him,* and to be sent out..." (*Mk* 3:13-14). The truth is that the interior call of the Spirit needs to be recognized as the authentic call of the Bishop. Just as all can *"go" to the Bishop,* because he is Shepherd and Father to all, his priests who share with him the one priesthood and ministry can do so in a special way: the Bishop, the Council tells us, should consider them and treat them as "brothers and friends".[202] By analogy the same can be said of those who are preparing for the priesthood. As for "being with him", with the Bishop, the Bishop should make a point of visiting them often and in some way "being" with them, as a way of giving significant expression to his responsibility for the formation of candidates for the priesthood.

The presence of the Bishop is especially valuable, not only because it helps the seminary community live its insertion in the particular Church and its communion with the Pastor who guides it, but also because it verifies and encourages the pastoral purpose which is what specifies the entire formation of candidates for the priesthood. In particular, with his presence and by his sharing with candidates for the priesthood all that has to do with the pastoral progress of the particular Church, the Bishop offers a fundamental contribution to formation in the "sensus Ecclesiae", as a central spiritual and pastoral value in the exercise of the priestly ministry.

The Seminary as an educational community

66. The educational community of the Seminary is built round the various people involved in

---

[202] Decree on the Ministry and Life of Priests *Presbyterorum Ordinis*, 7.

formation: the rector, the spiritual father or spiritual director, the superiors and professors. These people should feel profoundly united to the Bishop, whom they represent in their different roles and in various ways. They should also maintain among themselves a frank and genuine communion. The unity of the educators not only helps the educational programme to be put into practice properly, but also and above all it offers candidates for the priesthood a significant example and a practical introduction to that ecclesial communion which is a fundamental value of Christian living and of the pastoral ministry.

It is evident that much of the effectiveness of the training offered depends on the maturity and strength of personality of those entrusted with formation, both from the human and from the Gospel points of view. And so it is especially important, both *to select them carefully* and to encourage them to become ever *more suitable for carrying out the task entrusted* to them. The Synod Fathers were very aware that the future of the preparation of candidates for the priesthood depends on the choice and formation of those entrusted with the work of formation, and so they describe at length the qualities sought for in them. Specifically they wrote: "The task of formation of candidates for the priesthood requires not only a certain special preparation of those to whom this work is entrusted, one that is professional, pedagogical, spiritual, human and theological, but also a spirit of communion and of cooperating together to carry out the programme, so that the unity of the pastoral action of the Seminary is always maintained under the leadership of the rector. The body of formation personnel should witness to a truly evangelical lifestyle and total dedication to the Lord. It should enjoy a certain stability and its members as a rule should live in the Seminary community. They should be intimately joined to the Bishop, who is the first one responsible for the formation of the priests".[203]

The Bishops first of all should feel their grave responsibility for the formation of those who have been given the task of educating future priests. For this ministry, priests of exemplary life should be chosen, men with a number of qualities: "human and spiritual maturity, pastoral experience, professional competence, stability in their own vocation, a capacity to work with others, serious preparation in those human sciences (psychology especially) which relate to their office, a knowledge of how to work in groups".[204]

While safeguarding the distinctions between internal and external forum, and maintaining a suitable freedom in the choice of confessors and the prudence and discretion which should be a feature of the ministry of the spiritual director, the priestly community of teachers should feel united in the responsibility of educating candidates for the priesthood. It is their duty, always with regard

---

[203] *Propositio* 29.
[204] *Ibid.*

to the authoritative evaluation made by the Bishop and the rector together, to foster and verify in the first place the suitability of the candidates in regard to their spiritual, human and intellectual endowments, above all in regard to their spirit of prayer, their deep assimilation of the doctrine of the faith, their capacity for true fraternity and the charism of celibacy.[205]

Bearing in mind (as the Synod Fathers have indeed done) the indications of the Exhortation *Christifideles Laici*[206] and of the Apostolic Letter *Mulieris Dignitatem*, which stress the suitability of a healthy influence of lay spirituality and of the charism of femininity in every educational itinerary, it is worthwhile to involve, in ways that are prudent and adapted to the different cultural contexts, the cooperation also of *lay faithful, both men and women,* in the work of training future priests. They are to be selected with care, within the framework of Church laws and according to their particular charisms and proven competence. We can expect beneficial fruits from their cooperation, provided it is suitably coordinated and integrated in the primary educational responsibilities of those entrusted with the formation of future priests, fruits for a balanced growth of the sense of the Church and a more precise perception of what it is to be a priest on the part of the candidates to the priesthood.[207]

[205] Cf. *Propositio* 23.
[206] Cf. Post-Synodal Apostolic Exhortation *Christifideles Laici* (30 December 1988), 61; 63: *loc. cit.,* 512-514; 517-518; Apostolic Letter *Mulieris Dignitatem* (15 August 1988), 29-31: *loc. cit.,* 1721-1729.
[207] Cf. *Propositio* 29.

67.   Those who by their teaching of theology
introduce future priests to *sacred doctrine* and
accompany them in it have a particular educational responsibility. Experience teaches that
they often have a greater influence on the development of the priest's personality than other
educators.

The responsibility of the *teachers of theology*
will lead them, even before they consider the
teaching relationship they are to establish with
candidates for the priesthood, to look into the
concept they themselves should have of the nature
of theology and the priestly ministry, and also of
the spirit and style in which they should carry out
their teaching of theology. In this sense the Synod
Fathers have rightly affirmed that "the theologian
must never forget that as a teacher he is not presenting his personal doctrines but opening to and
communicating to others the understanding of the
faith, in the last analysis in the name of the Lord
and his Church. In such a way, the theologian,
using all the methods and techniques provided by
his science, carries out his task at the mandate
of the Church and cooperates with the Bishop
in his task of teaching. Since theologians and
Bishops are at the service of the Church herself in
promoting the faith, they should develop and
foster trust in each other and, in this spirit, overcome tensions and conflicts (for fuller treatment,
cf. Instruction of the Congregation for the Doc-

trine of the Faith on *The Ecclesial Vocation of the Theologian*)".[208]

The teacher of theology, like any other teacher, should remain in communion and sincerely cooperate with all the other people who are involved in the formation of future priests, and offer with scientific precision, generosity, humility and enthusiasm his own original and expert contribution, which is not simply the communication of doctrine—even though it be *sacred doctrine*—but is above all the presentation of the point of view which unifies, in the plan of God, all the different branches of human knowledge and the various expressions of life.

In particular, the formative effect of the teachers of theology will depend, above all, on whether they are "men of faith who are full of love for the Church, convinced that the one who really knows the Christian mystery is the Church as such and, therefore, that their task of teaching is really and truly an ecclesial ministry, men who have a richly developed pastoral sense which enables them to discern not only content but forms that are suitable for the exercise of their ministry. In particular, what is expected of the teachers is total fidelity to the Magisterium; for they teach in the name of the Church, and because of this they are witnesses to the faith.[209]

---

[208] *Propositio* 30.
[209] *Ibid.*

*Communities of origin and associations and youth
movements*

68.   The communities from which the candidate for the priesthood comes continue, albeit
with the necessary detachment which is involved
by the choice of a vocation, to bear considerable
influence on the formation of the future priest.
They should therefore be aware of their specific
share of responsibility.

Let us mention first of all the *family:* Christian
parents, as also brothers and sisters and the other
members of the family, should never seek to call
back the future priest within the narrow confines
of a too human (if not worldly) logic, no matter
how supported by sincere affection that logic may
be (cf. *Mk* 3:20-21, 31-35). Instead, driven by the
same desire "to fulfil the will of God", they
should accompany the formative journey with
prayer, respect, the good example of the domestic
virtues and spiritual and material help, especially
in difficult moments. Experience teaches that, in
so many cases, this multiple help has proved decisive for candidates for the priesthood. Even in the
case of parents or relatives who are indifferent or
opposed to the choice of a vocation, a clear and
calm facing of the situation and the encouragement which derives from it can be a great help to
the deeper and more determined maturing of a
priestly vocation.

Closely linked with the families is the *parish
community*. Both it and the family are connected

in education in the faith. Often, afterwards, the parish, with its specific pastoral care for young people and vocations, supplements the family's role. Above all, inasmuch as it is the most immediate local expression of the mystery of the Church, the parish offers an original and especially valuable contribution to the formation of a future priest. The parish community should continue to feel that the young man on his way to the priesthood is a living part of itself; it should accompany him with its prayer, give him a cordial welcome during the holiday periods, respect and encourage him to form himself in his identity as a priest, and offer him suitable opportunities and strong encouragement to try out his vocation for the priestly mission.

Associations and youth movements, which are a sign and confirmation of the vitality which the Spirit guarantees to the Church, can and should contribute also to the formation of candidates for the priesthood, in particular of those who are the product of the Christian, spiritual and apostolic experience of these groups. Young people who have received their basic formation in such groups and look to them for their experience of the Church should not feel they are being asked to uproot themselves from their past or to break their links with the environment which has contributed to their decision to respond to their vocation, nor should they erase the characteristic traits of the spirituality which they have learned and lived there, in all that they contain that is good, edifying and rich.[210] For them too, this environment from which they come continues to be a source of help and support on the path of formation towards the priesthood.

The Spirit offers to many young people opportunities to be educated in the faith and to grow as Christians and as members of the Church through many kinds of groups, movements and associations inspired in different ways by the Gospel message. These should be felt and lived as a nourishing gift of a soul within the institution and at its service. A movement or a particular spirituality "is not an alternative structure to the institution. It is rather a source of a presence which constantly regenerates the existential and historical authenticity of the institution. The priest should therefore find within a movement the light and warmth which make him capable of fidelity to his Bishop and which make him ready for the duties of the institution and mindful of ecclesiastical discipline, thus making the reality of his faith more fertile and his faithfulness more joyful".[211]

It is therefore necessary, in the new community of the Seminary in which they are gathered by the Bishop, that young people coming from associations and ecclesial movements should learn "respect for other spiritual paths and a spirit of dialogue and cooperation", should take in genuinely

<hr />

[210] Cf. *Propositio* 25.

[211] *Address* to priests connected with the "Communion and Liberation" movement (12 September 1985): *AAS* 78 (1986), 256.

and sincerely the indications for their training imparted by the Bishop and the teachers in the Seminary, abandoning themselves with real confidence to their guidance and assessments.[212] Such an attitude will prepare and in some way anticipate a genuine priestly choice to serve the entire People of God, in the fraternal communion of the presbyterate and in obedience to the Bishop.

The fact that seminarians and diocesan priests take part in particular spiritualities or ecclesial groupings is indeed, in itself, a factor which helps growth and priestly fraternity. Such participation, however, should not be an obstacle, but rather a help to the ministry and spiritual life which are proper to the diocesan priest, who "will always remain the shepherd of all. Not only is he a 'permanent' shepherd, available to all, but he presides over the gathering of all so that all may find the welcome which they have a right to expect in the community and in the Eucharist that unites them, whatever be their religious sensibility or pastoral commitment".[213]

The candidate himself

69.   Lastly, we must not forget that the candidate himself is a necessary and irreplaceable agent in his own formation: all formation, priestly formation included, is ultimately a self-formation. No

---

[212] Cf. *Propositio* 25.
[213] *Meeting* with members of the Swiss clergy, Einsiedeln (15 June 1984), 10: *Insegnamenti* VII/1 (1984), 1798.

one can replace us in the responsible freedom that we have as individual persons.

And so the future priest also, and in the first place, must grow in his awareness that the Agent par excellence of his formation is the Holy Spirit, who, by the gift of a new heart, configures and conforms him to Jesus Christ the Good Shepherd. In this way the candidate to the priesthood will affirm in the most radical way possible his freedom to welcome the moulding action of the Spirit. But to welcome this action implies also, on the part of the candidate, a welcome for the human "mediating" forces which the Spirit employs. As a result, the actions of the different teachers becomes truly and fully effective only if the future priest offers his own convinced and heartfelt cooperation to this work of formation.

CHAPTER VI

I REMIND YOU TO REKINDLE THE GIFT OF GOD THAT IS WITHIN YOU

THE ONGOING FORMATION OF PRIESTS

THEOLOGICAL REASONS BEHIND ONGOING FORMATION

70.   "I remind you to rekindle the gift of God that is within you" (*2 Tim* 1:6).

The words of Saint Paul to Timothy can appropriately be applied to the ongoing formation to which all priests are called by virtue of the "gift of God" which they have received at their ordination. The passage helps us to grasp the full truth, the absolute uniqueness of the permanent formation of priests. Here we are also helped by another text of Saint Paul, who once more writes to Timothy: "Do not neglect the gift you have, which was given you by prophetic utterance when the elders laid their hands upon you. Practise these duties, devote yourself to them, so that all may see your progress. Take heed to yourself and to your teaching; hold to that, for by so doing you will save both yourself and your hearers" (*1 Tim* 4:14-16).

Paul asks Timothy to "rekindle", or stir into

185

flame, the divine gift he has received, much as one might do with the embers of a fire, in the sense of welcoming it and living it out without ever losing or forgetting that "permanent novelty" which is characteristic of every gift from God, who makes all things new (cf. *Rev* 21:5), and thus living it out in its unfading freshness and original beauty.

But this "rekindling" is not only the outcome of a task entrusted to the personal responsibility of Timothy, nor only the result of his efforts to use his mind and will. It is also the effect of a dynamism of grace intrinsic to God's gift. God himself, in other words, rekindles his own gift, so as better to release all the extraordinary riches of grace and responsibility contained in it.

With the sacramental outpouring of the Holy Spirit who consecrates and sends forth, the priest is configured to the likeness of Jesus Christ, Head and Shepherd of the Church, and is sent forth to carry out a pastoral ministry. In this way the priest is marked permanently and indelibly in his inner being as a minister of Jesus and of the Church. He comes to share in a permanent and irreversible way of life and is entrusted with a pastoral ministry which, because it is rooted in his being and involves his entire life, is itself permanent. The Sacrament of Holy Orders confers upon the priest sacramental grace which gives him a share not only in Jesus' saving "power" and "ministry" but also in his pastoral "love". At the same time it ensures that the priest can count on all the actual graces he needs, whenever they are necessary and

186

useful for the worthy and perfect exercise of the ministry he has received.

We thus see that the proper foundation and original motivation for ongoing formation is contained in the dynamism of the Sacrament of Holy Orders.

Certainly there are also *purely human reasons* which call for the priest to engage in ongoing formation. This formation is demanded by his own continuing personal growth. Every life is a constant path towards maturity, a maturity which cannot be attained except by constant formation. It is also demanded by the priestly ministry seen in a general way and taken in common with other professions, that is as a service directed to others. There is no profession, job or work which does not require constant updating, if it is to remain current and effective. The need to "keep pace" with the path of history is another human reason justifying ongoing formation.

But these and other motivations are taken up and become even clearer by the *theological motivations* mentioned previously and which demand further reflection.

The *Sacrament of Holy Orders,* by its nature (common to all the sacraments) as a "sign", may be considered, and truly is, a *word of God.* It is a word of God which *calls and sends forth.* It is the strongest expression of the priest's vocation and mission. By the Sacrament of Holy Orders, *God calls the candidate "to" the priesthood "coram Ecclesia".* The "come, follow me" of Jesus is proclaimed fully and definitively in the sacramental celebration of his Church. It is made manifest and communicated by the Church's voice, which is heard in the words of the Bishop who prays and imposes his hands. The priest then gives his response, in faith, to Jesus's call: "I am coming, to follow you". From this moment there begins that response which, as a fundamental choice, must be expressed anew and reaffirmed through the years of his priesthood in countless other responses, all of them rooted in and enlivened by that "yes" of Holy Orders.

In this sense one can speak of a *vocation "within" the priesthood*. The fact is that God continues to call and send forth, revealing his saving plan in the historical development of the priest's life and the life of the Church and of society. It is in this perspective that the meaning of ongoing formation emerges. Permanent formation is necessary in order to discern and follow this constant call or will of God. Thus the Apostle Peter is called to follow Jesus even after the Risen Lord has entrusted his flock to him: "Jesus said to him, 'Feed my sheep. Truly, truly, I say to you, when you were young, you girded yourself and walked where you would; but when you are old, you will stretch out your hands, and another will gird you and carry you where you do not wish to go.' (This he said to show by what death he was to glorify God.) And after this he said to him, 'Follow me'" (*Jn* 21:17-19). Consequently there is a "follow me" which accompanies the Apostle's whole life and mission. It is a "follow me" in line with the call and demand of *faithfulness unto death*

188

(cf. *Jn* :22), a "follow me" which can signify a *sequela Christi* to the point of total self-giving in martyrdom.[214]

The Synod Fathers explained the reason justifying the need for ongoing formation, while at the same time revealing its deep nature, as *"faithfulness"* to the *priestly ministry* and as a *"process of continual conversion"*.[215] It is the Holy Spirit, poured out in the Sacrament, who sustains the priest in this faithfulness and accompanies him and encourages him along this path of unending conversion. The gift of the Spirit does not take away the freedom of the priest. It calls on the priest to make use of his freedom in order to cooperate responsibly and accept permanent formation as a task entrusted to him. Thus permanent formation is a requirement of the priest's own faithfulness to his ministry, to his very being. It is love for Jesus Christ and fidelity to oneself. But it is also an *act of love for the People of God,* at whose service the priest is placed. Indeed, an act of *true and proper justice:* the priest owes it to God's People, whose fundamental "right" to receive the word of God, the sacraments and the service of charity, the original and irreplaceable content of the priest's own pastoral ministry, he is called to acknowledge and foster. Ongoing formation is necessary to ensure that the priest can properly respond to this right of the People of God.

The heart and form of the priest's ongoing forma-

---

[214] Cf. Saint Augustine, *In Iohannis Evangelium Tractatus* 123, 5: *loc. cit.,* 678-680.
[215] Cf. *Propositio* 31.

tion is pastoral charity: the Holy Spirit, who infuses pastoral charity, introduces and accompanies the priest to an ever deeper knowledge of the mystery of Christ which is unfathomable in its richness (cf. *Eph* 3:14ff.) and, in turn, to a knowledge of the mystery of Christian priesthood. Pastoral charity itself impels the priest to an ever deeper knowledge of the hopes, the needs, the problems, the sensibilities of the people to whom he ministers, taken in their specific situations, as individuals, in their families, in society, and in history.

All this constitutes the object of ongoing formation, understood as a conscious and free decision to live out the dynamism of pastoral charity and of the Holy Spirit who is its first source and constant nourishment. In this sense, ongoing formation is an intrinsic requirement of the gift and sacramental ministry received; and it proves necessary in every age. It is particularly urgent today, not only because of rapid changes in the social and cultural conditions of individuals and peoples among whom priestly ministry is exercised, but also because of that "new evangelization" which constitutes the essential and pressing task of the Church at the end of the Second Millennium.

DIFFERENT DIMENSIONS OF ONGOING FORMATION

71.   The ongoing formation of priests, whether diocesan or religious, is the natural and absolutely necessary continuation of the process of building priestly personality which began and developed in

the Seminary or the Religious House with the training programme which aimed at ordination.

It is particularly important to be aware of and to respect the intrinsic *link between formation before ordination to the Priesthood and formation after ordination*. Should there be a break in continuity, or worse, a complete difference between these two phases of formation, there would be serious and immediate repercussions on pastoral work and fraternal communion among priests, especially those in different age groups. Ongoing formation is not a repetition of the formation acquired in the Seminary, simply reviewed or expanded with new and practical suggestions. Ongoing formation involves relatively new content and especially methods; it develops as a harmonious and vital process which—rooted in the formation received in the Seminary—calls for adaptations, updating and modifications, but without sharp breaks in continuity.

On the other hand, long-term preparation for ongoing formation should take place in the Major Seminary, where encouragement needs to be given to future priests to look forward to it, seeing its necessity, its advantages and the spirit in which it should be undertaken, and appropriate conditions for its realization need to be ensured.

By the very fact that ongoing formation is a continuation of the formation received in the Seminary, its aim cannot be the inculcation of a purely "professional" approach, which could be acquired by learning a few new pastoral techniques. Instead its aim must be that of promoting a general and integral process of constant growth, deepening each of the aspects of formation—human, spiritual, intellectual and pastoral—as well as ensuring their active and harmonious integration, based on pastoral charity and in reference to it.

72.   Fuller development is first required in the *human aspect* of priestly formation. Through his daily contact with people, his sharing in their daily lives, the priest needs to develop and sharpen his human sensitivity so as to understand more clearly their needs, respond to their demands, perceive their unvoiced questions, and share the hopes and expectations, the joys and burdens which are part of life: thus he will be able to meet and enter into dialogue with all people. In particular, through coming to know and share, through making his own, the human experience of suffering in its many different manifestations, from poverty to illness, from rejection to ignorance, loneliness, and material or moral poverty, the priest can cultivate his own humanity and make it all the more genuine and clearly apparent by his increasingly ardent love for his fellow man.

In this task of bringing his human formation to maturity, the priest receives special assistance from the grace of Jesus Christ. The charity of the Good Shepherd was revealed not only by his gift of salvation to mankind, but also by his desire to share our life: thus, the Word who became "flesh" (cf. *Jn* 1:14) desired to know joy and suffering, to experience weariness, to share feelings, to console sadness. Living as a man among and with men, Jesus Christ offers the most complete, genuine and perfect expression of what it means to be human. We see him celebrating at the wedding feast of Cana, a friend's family, moved by the hungry crowd who follow him, giving sick or even dead children back to their parents, weeping for the death of Lazarus, and so on.

The People of God should be able to say about the priest, who has increasingly matured in human sensitivity, something similar to what we read about Jesus in the Letter to the Hebrews: "For we have not a high priest who is unable to sympathize with our weaknesses, but one who in every respect has been tempted as we are, yet without sinning" (*Heb* 4:15).

The formation of the priest in its *spiritual dimension* is required by the new Gospel life to which he has been called in a specific way by the Holy Spirit, poured out in the Sacrament of Holy Orders. The Spirit, by consecrating the priest and configuring him to Jesus Christ, Head and Shepherd, creates a bond which, located in the priest's very being, demands to be assimilated and lived out in a personal, free and conscious way through an ever richer communion of life and love and an ever broader and more radical sharing in the feelings and attitudes of Jesus Christ. In this bond between the Lord Jesus and the priest, an ontological and psychological bond, a sacramental and moral bond, is the foundation and likewise the power for that "life according to the Spirit" and that "radicalism of the Gospel" to which every priest is called today and which is fostered by on-going formation in its spiritual aspect. This formation proves necessary also for the priestly ministry to be genuine and spiritually fruitful. "Are you exercising the care of souls?", Saint Charles Borromeo once asked in a talk to priests. And he went on to say: "Do not thereby neglect yourself. Do not give yourself to others to such an extent that nothing is left of yourself for yourself. You should certainly keep in mind the souls whose pastor you are, but without forgetting yourself. My brothers, do not forget that there is nothing so necessary to all churchmen than the meditation which precedes, accompanies and follows all our actions: I will sing, says the Prophet, and I will meditate (cf. *Ps* 100:1). If you administer the sacraments, my brother, meditate upon what you are doing. If you celebrate Mass, meditate on what you are offering. If you recite the Psalms in choir, meditate to whom and of what you are speaking. If you are guiding souls, meditate in whose blood they have been cleansed. And let all be done among you in charity (*1 Cor* 16:14). Thus we will be able to overcome the difficulties we meet, countless as they are, each day. In any event, this is what is demanded of us by the task entrusted to us. If we act thus, we will find the strength to give birth to Christ in ourselves and in others".[216]

The priest's prayer life in particular needs to be continually "re-formed". Experience teaches

---

[216] SAINT CHARLES BORROMEO, *Acta Ecclesiae Mediolanensis,* Milan 1599, 1178.

that in prayer one cannot live off past gains. Every day, we need not only to renew our external fidelity to times of prayer, especially those devoted to the celebration of the Liturgy of the Hours and those left to personal choice and not reinforced by fixed times of liturgical service, but also to strive constantly for the experience of a genuine personal encounter with Jesus, a trusting dialogue with the Father, and a deep experience of the Spirit.

What the Apostle Paul says of all Christians, that they must attain "to mature manhood, to the measure of the stature of the fulness of Christ" (*Eph* 4:13), can be applied specifically to priests, who are called to the perfection of charity and therefore to holiness, even more so because their pastoral ministry itself demands that they be living models for all the faithful.

The *intellectual dimension* of formation likewise needs to be continually fostered through the priest's entire life, especially by a commitment to study and a serious and disciplined familiarity with modern culture. As one who shares in the prophetic mission of Jesus and is part of the mystery of the Church the Teacher of truth, the priest is called to reveal to others, in Jesus Christ, the true face of God, and as a result the true face of man.[217] This demands that the priest himself seek God's face and contemplate it with loving veneration (cf. *Ps* 26:7; 41:2). Only thus will he be able to make others know him. In particular, continu-

---

[217] Cf. SECOND VATICAN ECUMENICAL COUNCIL, Pastoral Constitution on the Church in the Modern World *Gaudium et Spes*, 22.

ing theological study is necessary if the priest is to faithfully carry out the ministry of the word, proclaiming it clearly and without ambiguity, distinguishing it from mere human opinions, no matter how renowned and widespread these might be. Thus he will be able to stand at the service of the People of God, helping them to give an account, to all who ask, of their Christian hope (cf. *1 Pt* 3:15). Furthermore, the priest "in applying himself conscientiously and diligently to theological study, is in a position to asimilate the genuine richness of the Church in a sure and personal way. Therefore, he can faithfully discharge the mission which is incumbent on him when responding to difficulties about authentic Catholic doctrine, and overcome the inclination, both in himself and others, which leads to dissent and negative attitudes towards the Magisterium and Sacred Tradition".[218]

The *pastoral aspect* of ongoing formation is well expressed by the words of the Apostle Peter: "As each has received a gift, employ it for one another, as good stewards of God's varied grace" (*1 Pt* 4:10). If he is to live daily according to the graces he has received, the priest must be ever more open to accepting the pastoral charity of Jesus Christ granted him by Christ's Spirit in the Sacrament he has received. Just as all the Lord's activity was the fruit and sign of pastoral charity, so should the priest's ministerial activity be. Pastoral charity is a gift, but it is likewise a task, a

[218] SYNOD OF BISHOPS, Ordinary General Assembly, "The Formation of Priests in the Circumstances of the Present Day", *Instrumentum Laboris,* 55.

grace and a responsibility to which we must be faithful. We have, therefore, to welcome it and live out its dynamism even to its most radical demands. This pastoral charity, as has been said, impels the priest and stimulates him to become ever better acquainted with the real situation of the men and women to whom he is sent, to discern the call of the Spirit in the historical circumstances in which he finds himself, and to seek the most suitable methods and the most useful forms for carrying out his ministry today. Thus pastoral charity encourages and sustains the priest's human efforts for pastoral activity that is relevant, credible and effective. But this demands some kind of permanent pastoral formation.

The path towards maturity does not simply demand that the priest deepen the different aspects of his formation. It also demands above all that he be able to combine ever more harmoniously all these aspects, gradually achieving their *inner unity*. This will be made possible by pastoral charity. Indeed, pastoral charity not only coordinates and unifies the diverse aspects, but it makes them more specific, marking them out as aspects of the formation of the priest as such, that is of the priest as a clear and living image, a minister of Jesus the Good Shepherd.

Ongoing formation helps the priest to overcome the temptation to reduce his ministry to an activism which becomes an end in itself, to the provision of impersonal services, even if these are spiritual or sacred, or to a business-like function which he carries out for the Church. Only ongoing formation enables the priest to *safeguard with vigilant love the "mystery" which he bears within his heart for the good of the Church and of mankind.*

THE PROFOUND MEANING OF ONGOING FORMATION

73. The different and complementary dimensions of ongoing formation help us to grasp its profound meaning. Ongoing formation helps the priest to *be* and *act* as a priest in the spirit and style of Jesus the Good Shepherd.

Truth needs to be put into practice! St James tells us as much: "Be doers of the word, and not hearers only, deceiving yourselves" (*Jas* 1:22). Priests are called to "live the truth" of their being, that is to live "in love" (cf. *Eph* 4:15) their identity and ministry in the Church and for the Church. They are called to become ever more aware of the gift of God, and to live it out constantly. This is the invitation Paul makes to Timothy: "Guard the truth that has been entrusted to you by the Holy Spirit who dwells within us" (*2 Tim* 1:14).

In the ecclesiological context which we have recalled more than once, we can consider the profound meaning of ongoing priestly formation in relation to the priest's presence and activity in the Church as *mysterium, communio et missio.*

Within the Church as "mystery" the priest is called, by his ongoing formation, to *safeguard and develop in faith his awareness of the total and marvel-*

lous truth of his being: he is a minister of Christ and steward of the mysteries of God (cf. *1 Cor* 4:1). Paul expressly asks Christians to consider him in this way. But even before that, he himself lives in the awareness of the sublime gift he has received from the Lord. This should be the case with every priest, if he wishes to remain true to his being. But this is possible only in faith, only by looking at things through the eyes of Christ.

In this sense it can be said that ongoing formation has as its aim that *the priest become a believer and ever more of one:* that he grow in understanding of who he truly is, seeing things with the eyes of Christ. The priest must safeguard this truth with grateful and joyful love. He must renew his faith when he exercises his priestly ministry; he must feel himself a minister of Christ, a sacrament of the love of God for mankind, every time that he is the means and the living instrument for conferring God's grace upon men. He must recognize this same truth in his fellow priests, for this is the basis of his respect and love for other priests.

74.   Ongoing formation helps priests, *within the Church as "communion",* to deepen their awareness that their ministry is ultimately aimed at gathering together the family of God as a brotherhood inspired by charity and to lead it to the Father through Christ in the Holy Spirit.[219]

The priest should grow in *awareness of the deep communion uniting him to the People of God:*

---

[219] Cf. SECOND VATICAN ECUMENICAL COUNCIL, Decree on the Ministry and Life of Priests *Presbyterorum Ordinis,* 6.

199

he is not only "in the forefront of" the Church, but above all "in" the Church. He is a brother among brothers. By Baptism, which marks him with the dignity and freedom of the children of God in the only-begotten Son, the priest is a member of the one Body of Christ (cf. *Eph* 4:16). His consciousness of this communion leads to a need to awaken and deepen *co-responsibility* in the one common mission of salvation, with a prompt and heartfelt esteem for all the charisms and tasks which the Spirit gives believers for the building up of the Church. It is above all in the exercise of the pastoral ministry, directed by its very nature to the good of the People of God, that the priest must live and give witness to his profound communion with all. As Pope Paul VI wrote: "We must become brothers to all at the very same time as we wish to be their shepherds, fathers and teachers. The climate of dialogue is friendship. Indeed it is service".[220]

More specifically, the priest is called to deepen his awareness of being a *member of the particular Church* in which he is incardinated, joined by a bond that is juridical, spiritual and pastoral. This awareness presupposes a particular love for his own Church and it makes that love grow. This is truly the living and permanent goal of the pastoral charity which should accompany the life of the priest and lead him to share in the history or life-experience of this same particular Church, in its

---

[220] PAUL VI, Encyclical Letter *Ecclesiam suam* (6 August 1964), III: *AAS* 56 (1964), 647.

riches and in its weaknesses, in its difficulties and in its hopes, working in it for its growth. And thus to feel himself both enriched by the particular Church and actively involved in building it up, carrying on—as an individual and together with others priests—that pastoral involvement typical of his brother priests who have gone before him. A necessary requirement of this pastoral charity towards one's own particular Church and its future ministry is the concern which the priest should have to find, so to speak, someone to replace him in the priesthood.

The priest must grow in his awareness of the *communion existing between the various particular Churches,* a communion rooted in their very being as Churches which make present in various places Christ's one universal Church. This awareness of the communion of the particular Churches will foster an *"exchange of gifts",* beginning with living and personal gifts, such as priests themselves. There should be a readiness, indeed a generous commitment, to provide for a fair distribution of clergy.[221] Among these particular Churches, those should be kept in mind which, because they are "deprived of freedom, cannot have their own vocations", as well as those "Churches which have emerged recently from persecution and poor Churches which have been given help already for

---

[221] Cf. SACRED CONGREGATION FOR THE CLERGY, Directives for the promotion of mutual cooperation between particular Churches and especially for a more suitable distribution of the clergy *Postquam Apostoli* (25 March 1980): *AAS* 72 (1980), 343-364.

many years and from many sources with great-hearted brotherliness, and still receive help".[222]

Within the ecclesial communion, the priest is called in particular to *grow,* thanks to his ongoing formation, *in and with his own presbyterate in union with his Bishop.* The presbyterate, in the fullness of its truth, is a *mysterium:* it is in fact a supernatural reality because it is rooted in the Sacrament of Holy Orders. This is its source and origin. This is its "place" of birth and of its growth. Indeed, "priests by means of the Sacrament of Orders are tied with a personal and indissoluble bond to Christ the one priest. The Sacrament of Holy Orders is conferred upon each of them as individuals, but they are inserted into the communion of the presbyterate united with the Bishop (*Lumen Gentium,* 28; *Presbyterorum Ordinis,* 7 and 8)".[223]

This sacramental origin is reflected and continued in the sphere of priestly ministry: from *mysterium* to *ministerium.* "Unity among the priests with the Bishop and among themselves is not something added from the outside to the nature of their service, but expresses its essence inasmuch as it is the care of Christ the priest for the People gathered in the unity of the Blessed Trinity".[224] This unity among priests, lived in a spirit of pastoral charity, makes priests witnesses of Jesus Christ, who prayed to the Father "that they may all be one" (*Jn* 17:21).

The presbyterate thus appears as a *true family,*

---

[222] *Propositio* 39.
[223] *Propositio* 34.
[224] *Ibid.*

as a fraternity whose ties do not arise from flesh and blood but from the grace of Holy Orders. This grace takes up and elevates the human and psychological bonds of affection and friendship, as well as the spiritual bonds which exist between priests. It is a grace that grows ever greater and finds expression in the most varied forms of mutual assistance, spiritual and material as well. Priestly fraternity excludes no one. However it can and should have its preferences, those of the Gospel, reserved for those who have greatest need of help and encouragement. This fraternity "takes special care of the young priests, maintains a kind and fraternal dialogue with those of the middle and older age groups, and with those who for whatever reasons are facing difficulties; as for those priests who have given up this way of life or are not following it at this time, this brotherhood does not forget them but follows them all the more with fraternal solicitude".[225]

Religious clergy who live and work in a particular Church also belong to the one presbyterate, albeit under a different title. Their presence is a source of enrichment for all priests. The different particular charisms which they live, while challenging all priests to grow in the understanding of the priesthood itself, help to encourage and promote ongoing priestly formation. The gift of religious life, in the framework of the Diocese, when accompanied by genuine esteem and rightful respect for the particular features of each Institute and

---

[225] *Ibid.*

each spiritual tradition, broadens the horizon of Christian witness and contributes in various ways to an enrichment of priestly spirituality, above all with regard to the proper relationship and interplay between the values of the particular Church and those of the whole People of God. For their part, Religious will be concerned to ensure a spirit of true ecclesial communion, a genuine participation in the progress of the Diocese and the pastoral decisions of the Bishop, generously putting their own charism at the service of building up everyone in charity.[226]

Finally, it is in the context of the Church as communion and in the context of the presbyterate that we can best discuss the problem of *priestly loneliness* treated by the Synod Fathers. There is a loneliness which all priests experience and which is completely normal. But there is another loneliness which is the product of various difficulties and which in turn creates further difficulties. With regard to the latter, "active participation in the diocesan presbyterate, regular contact with the Bishop and with the other priests, mutual cooperation, common life or fraternal dealings between priests, as also friendship and good relations with the lay faithful who are active in parish life, are very useful means to overcome the negative effects

---

[226] Cf. *Propositio* 38; SECOND VATICAN ECUMENICAL COUNCIL, Decree on the Ministry and Life of Priests *Presbyterorum Ordinis,* 1; Decree on Priestly Formation *Optatam Totius,* 1; SACRED CONGREGATION FOR RELIGIOUS AND SECULAR INSTITUTES and SACRED CONGREGATION FOR BISHOPS, Directives for mutual relations between Bishops and Religious in the Church *Mutuae Relationes* (14 May 1978), 2; 10: *loc. cit.,* 475; 479-480.

of loneliness which the priest can sometimes experience".[227]

Loneliness does not however create only difficulties; it can also offer positive opportunities for the priestly life: "when it is accepted in a spirit of oblation and is seen as an opportunity for greater intimacy with Jesus Christ the Lord, solitude can be an opportunity for prayer and study, as also a help for sanctification and also for human growth".[228]

It should be added that a certain type of solitude is a necessary element in ongoing formation. Jesus often went off alone to pray (cf. *Mt* 14:23). The ability to handle a healthy solitude is indispensable for caring for one's interior life. Here we are speaking of a solitude filled with the presence of the Lord who puts us in contact with the Father, in the light of the Spirit. In this regard, concern for silence and looking for places and times of "desert" are necessary for the priest's permanent formation, whether in the intellectual, spiritual or pastoral areas. In this regard too, it can be said that those unable to have a positive experience of their own solitude are incapable of genuine and fraternal fellowship.

75. Ongoing formation aims at *increasing the priest's awareness of his share in the Church's saving mission*. In the Church's "mission", the priest's permanent formation appears not only as a necessary condition but also as an indispensable means for constantly refocusing on the *meaning* of his

---

[227] *Propositio* 35.
[228] *Ibid.*

205

mission and for ensuring that he is carrying it out with fidelity and generosity. By this formation, the priest is helped to become aware of the seriousness and yet the splendid grace of an obligation which cannot let him rest, so that, like Paul, he must be able to say: "If I preach the Gospel, that gives me no ground for boasting. For necessity is laid upon me. Woe to me if I do not preach the Gospel!" (*1 Cor* 9:16). At the same time, he also becomes aware of a demand, whether explicit or implicit, which insistently comes from all those whom God is unceasingly calling to salvation.

Only a suitable ongoing formation will succeed in confirming the priest in the essential and decisive element in his ministry, namely his faithfulness. The Apostle Paul writes: "it is required of stewards (of the mysteries of God) that they be found trustworthy" (*1 Cor* 4:2). The priest must be faithful no matter how many and varied the difficulties he meets, even in the most uncomfortable situations or when he is understandably tired, expending all his available energy until the end of his life. Paul's witness should be both an example and an incentive for every priest: "We put no obstacle—he writes to the Christians at Corinth—in any one's way, so that no fault may be found with our ministry, but as servants of God we commend ourselves in every way: through great endurance, in afflictions, hardships, calamities, beatings, imprisonments, tumults, labours, watching, hunger; by purity, knowledge, forbearance, kindness, the Holy Spirit, genuine love, truthful speech, and the power of God; with

206

the weapons of righteousness for the right hand and for the left; in honour and dishonour, in ill repute and good repute. We are treated as impostors, and yet are true; as unknown, and yet well known; as dying, and behold, we live; as punished, and yet not killed; as sorrowful, yet always rejoicing; as poor, yet making many rich; as having nothing, and yet possessing everything" (2 *Cor* 6:3-10).

AT EVERY AGE AND IN ALL CONDITIONS OF LIFE

76.   Permanent or ongoing formation, precisely because it is "permanent", should *always* be a part of the priest's life. In every phase and condition of his life, at every level of responsibility he has in the Church, he is underdoing formation. Clearly then, the possibilities for formation and the different kinds of formation are connected with the variety of ages, conditions of life and duties one finds among priests.

Ongoing formation is a duty, in the first instance, for *young priests*. They should have frequent and systematic meetings which, while they continue the sound and serious formation they have received in the Seminary, will gradually lead young priests to grasp and incarnate the unique wealth of God's gift which is the priesthood and to express their capabilities and ministerial attitude, also through an ever more convinced and responsible insertion in the presbyterate, and therefore in communion and co-responsibility with all their brethren.

With priests who have just come out of the Seminary, a certain sense of "having had enough" is quite understandable, when faced with new times of study and meeting. But the idea that priestly formation ends on the day one leaves the Seminary is false and dangerous, and needs to be totally rejected.

Young priests who take part in meetings for ongoing formation will be able to help one another by exchanging experiences and reflecting on how to put into practice the ideals of the priesthood and of ministry which they have imbibed during their Seminary years. At the same time, their active participation in the formational meetings of the presbyterate can be an example and stimulus to other priests who are ahead of them in years. They can thus show their love for all those making up the presbyterate and how much they care for their particular Church, which needs well formed priests.

In order to accompany the young priests in this first delicate phase of their life and ministry, it is very opportune, and perhaps even absolutely necessary nowadays, to create *a suitable support structure,* with appropriate guides and teachers. Here priests can find, in an organized way that continues through their first years of ministry, the help they need to make a good start in their priestly service. Through frequent and regular meetings—of sufficient duration and held within a community setting, if possible—they will be assured of having times for rest, prayer, reflection and fraternal exchange. It will then be easier for them, right from the beginning, to give a balanced approach, based on the Gospel, to their priestly life. And in those cases where individual local Churches are not in a position to offer this service to their own young priests, it will be a good idea for neighbouring Churches to pool resources and draw up suitable programmes.

77.　　Ongoing formation is a duty also for *priests of middle age.* They can face a number of risks, precisely because of their age, as for example, an exaggerated activism or a certain routine approach to the exercise of their ministry. As a result, the priest can be tempted to presume he can manage on his own, as if his own personal experience, which has seemed trustworthy to that point, needs no contact with anything or anyone else. Often enough, the older priest has a sort of interior fatigue which is dangerous. It can be a sign of a resigned disillusionment in the face of difficulties and failures. Such situations find an answer in ongoing formation, in a continued and balanced checking of oneself and one's activity, constantly looking for motivation and aids which will enable one to carry on one's mission. As a result the priest will maintain a vigilant spirit, ready to face the perennial yet ever new demands of salvation which people keep bringing to him as the "man of God".

Ongoing formation should also involve those *priests* who by their advanced years can be called *elderly* and who in some Churches make up the greater part of the presbyterate. The presbyterate should show them gratitude for the faithful service they have performed on behalf of Christ and his Church, and also practical solidarity to help them in their condition. Ongoing formation for these priests will not be a matter so much of study, updating and educational renewal, but rather a calm and reassuring confirmation of the part which they are still called upon to play in the presbyterate, not only inasmuch as they continue, perhaps in different ways, their pastoral ministry, but also because of the possibilities they themselves have, thanks to their experience of life and apostolate, of becoming effective teachers and trainers of other priests.

Also those priests who, because of the burden of work or illness, find themselves in a *condition of physical weakness or moral fatigue* can be helped by an ongoing formation which will encourage them to keep up their service to the Church in a calm and sustained fashion, and not to isolate themselves either from the community or from the presbyterate. However, they should reduce their external activities and dedicate themselves to those pastoral contacts and that personal spirituality which can help them keep up their motivation and priestly joy. Ongoing formation will help such priests to keep alive the conviction, which they themselves have inculcated in the faithful, that they continue to be active members for the building up of the Church, especially by virtue of their union with the suffering Christ and with so many other brothers and sisters in the Church who are sharing in the Lord's Passion, reliving Paul's spiritual experience when he said, "I rejoice in my sufferings for your sake, and in my flesh I complete what is lacking in Christ's afflictions for the sake of his body, that is, the church" (*Col* 1:24).[229]

THE AGENTS OF ONGOING FORMATION

78.   The conditions in which the ministry of priests often and in many places has to be carried out nowadays do not make it easy to undertake a serious commitment to formation. The multiplication of responsibilities and services, the complexity of human life in general and the life of the Christian communities in particular, the activism and anxiety that are features of vast areas of society today often deprive priests of the time and energies they need to "take heed of themselves" (cf. *1 Tim* 4:16).

This should increase the responsibility of priests to overcome these difficulties and see them as a challenge to plan and carry out a permanent formation which will respond appropriately to the greatness of God's gift and to the urgency of the demands and requirements of our time.

Those responsible for the ongoing formation of priests are to be found in the Church as "communion". In this sense, the *entire particular Church* has the responsibility, under the guidance of the Bishop, to develop and look after the different

[229] Cf. *Propositio* 36.

aspects of her priests' permanent formation. Priests are not there to serve themselves but the People of God. So, ongoing formation, in ensuring the human, spiritual, intellectual and pastoral maturity of priests, is doing good to the People of God itself. Besides, the very exercise of the pastoral ministry leads to a constant and fruitful mutual exchange between the priest's life of faith and that of the laity. Indeed *the very relationship and sharing of life between the priest and the community,* if it is wisely conducted and made use of, will be a *fundamental contribution* to permanent formation, which cannot be reduced to isolated episodes or initiatives, but covers the whole ministry and life of the priest.

The truth is that the Christian experience of persons who are simple and humble, the spiritual enthusiasm of people who truly love God, the courageous application of the faith to practical life by Christians involved in all kinds of social and civil tasks—all these things are embraced by the priest who, while illuminating them with his priestly service, at the same time draws from them a precious spiritual nourishment. Even the doubts, crises and hesitations in the face of all kinds of personal or social situations, the temptation to rejection or despair at times of pain, illness, death: all the difficult circumstances which people find in their path as Christians are fraternally lived and sincerely suffered in the priest's heart. And he, in seeking answers for others, is constantly spurred on to find them first of all for himself.

212

And so the entire People of God, in each and every one of its members, can and should offer precious assistance to the ongoing formation of its priests. In this sense the people should see that priests are allowed time for study and prayer. They should ask of them that for which Christ has sent them and not require anything else. They should offer to help in the various aspects of the pastoral mission, especially in those related to human development and works of charity. They should establish cordial and brotherly relations with them, helping priests to remember that they are not "to lord it over" the faithful, but rather "work with them for their joy" (cf. *2 Cor* 1: 24).

The particular Church's responsibility for the formation of its priests is specific and depends on its different members, starting with the priest himself.

79.   In a certain sense, it is the priest himself, *the individual priest, who is the person primarily responsible in the Church for ongoing formation.* Truly each priest has the duty, rooted in the Sacrament of Holy Orders, to be faithful to the gift God has given him and to respond to the call for daily conversion which comes with the gift itself. The regulations and norms established by Church authority, as also the example given by other priests, are not enough to make permanent formation attractive unless the individual priest is personally convinced of its need and is determined to make use of the opportunities, times and forms in which it comes. Ongoing formation

213

keeps up one's "youthfulness" of spirit, which is something that cannot be imposed from without. Each priest must continually find it within himself. Only those who keep ever alive their desire to learn and grow can be said to enjoy this "youthfulness".

The responsibility of the *Bishop* and, with him, of the *presbyterate,* is fundamental. The Bishop's responsibility is based on the fact that priests receive their priesthood from him and share his pastoral solicitude for the People of God. He is responsible for ongoing formation, the purpose of which is to ensure that all his priests are generously faithful to the gift and ministry received, that they are priests such as the People of God wishes to have and has a "right" to. This responsibility leads the Bishop, in communion with the presbyterate, to outline a project and establish a programme which can ensure that ongoing formation is not something haphazard but a systematic offering of subjects, which unfold by stages and take on precise forms. The Bishop will live up to his responsibility, not only by seeing to it that his presbyterate has places and times for its ongoing formation, but also by being present in person and taking part in an interested and friendly way. Often it will be suitable, or indeed necessary, for Bishops of neighbouring dioceses or of an ecclesiastical region to come together and join forces to be able to offer initiatives for permanent formation that are better organized and more interesting, such as in-service training courses in biblical, theological and pastoral studies, residential weeks, conference series, and times to reflect on and examine how, from the pastoral point of view, the affairs of the presbyterate and the ecclesial community are progressing.

To fulfil his responsibility in this field, the Bishop will also ask for help from theological and pastoral faculties or institutes, seminaries, offices and federations that bring together people—priests, religious and lay faithful—who are involved in priestly formation.

In the context of the particular Churches, *families* have a significant role to play. The life of ecclesial communities, led and guided by priests, looks to families inasmuch as they are "domestic churches". In particular the role of the family into which the priest is born needs to be stressed. By being one with their son in his aims, the family can offer him its own important contribution to his mission. The plan of Providence chose the priest's family to be the place in which his vocation was planted and nourished, an indispensible help for the growth and development of his vocation. Now the family, with the greatest respect for their son who has chosen to give himself to God and neighbour, should always remain as a faithful and encouraging witness of his mission, supporting that mission and sharing in it with devotion and respect. In this way the family will help bring God's providential plan to completion.

80.   While every moment can be an "acceptable time" (*2 Cor* 6:2) for the Holy Spirit to lead the priest to a direct growth in prayer, study and an awareness of his own pastoral responsibilities, nevertheless there are certain "privileged" moments for this, even though they may be common and prearranged.

Let us recall, in the first place, *the meetings of the Bishop with his presbyterate,* whether they be liturgical (in particular the concelebration of the Chrism Mass on Holy Thursday), or pastoral and educational, related to pastoral activity or to the study of specific theological problems.

There are also *spiritual gatherings for priests,* such as spiritual exercises, days of recollection and spirituality, etc. These are opportunities for spiritual and pastoral growth, in which one can devout more time to pray in peace; opportunities to get back to the what it means deep down to be a priest, to find fresh motives for faithfulness and pastoral endeavour.

Study workshops and sessions for reflection in common are also important. They help to prevent cultural impoverishment or getting entrenched in one's ways, even in the pastoral field, as a result of mental laziness. They help to foster a greater synthesis between the various elements of the spiritual, intellectual and apostolic life. They open minds and hearts to the new challenges of history and to the new appeals which the Spirit addresses to the Church.

81.   Many ways and means are at hand to make ongoing formation an ever more precious living experience for priests. Among them, let us recall the different *forms of common life* among priests, which have always existed, though they have appeared in different ways and with different degrees of intensity, in the life of the Church: "Today, it is impossible not to recommend them, especially among those who live together or are pastorally involved in the same place. Besides the advantage which comes to the apostolate and its activities, this common life of priests offers to all, to fellow priests and lay faithful alike, a shining example of charity and unity".[230]

Another help can be given by *priestly associations,* in particular by priestly secular institutes—which have as their characteristic feature their being diocesan—through which priests are more closely united to their Bishop, and which constitute "a state of consecration in which priests by means of vows or other sacred bonds consecrate themselves to incarnate in their life the evangelical counsels".[231] All the forms of "priestly fraternity" approved by the Church are useful not

[230] SYNOD OF BISHOPS, 8th Ordinary General Assembly, "The Formation of Priests in the Circumstances of the Present Day", *Instrumentum Laboris,* 60; cf. SECOND VATICAN ECUMENICAL COUNCIL, Decree on the Pastoral Office of Bishops in the Church *Christus Dominus,* 30; Decree on the Ministry and Life of Priests *Presbyterorum Ordinis,* 8; *C.I.C.,* can. 550 § 2.
[231] *Propositio* 37.

only for the spiritual life but also for the apostolic and pastoral life.

Spiritual direction too contributes in no small way to the ongoing formation of the priests. It is a well-tried means and has lost none of its value. It ensures spiritual formation. It fosters and maintains faithfulness and generosity in the carrying out of the priestly ministry. As Pope Paul VI wrote before his election to the Pontificate: "Spiritual direction has a wonderful purpose. We could say it is indispensable for the moral and spiritual education of young people who want to find what their vocation in life is and follow it wherever it may lead, with utter loyalty. It retains its beneficial effect at all stages of life, when in the light and affection of a devout and prudent counsel one asks for a check on one's own right intention and for support in the generous fulfilment of one's own duties. It is a very delicate but immensely valuable psychological means. It is an educational and psychological art calling for deep responsibility in the one who practises it. Whereas for the one who receives it, it is a spiritual act of humility and trust". [232]

---

[232] G.B. MONTINI, Pastoral Letter on the Moral Sense, 1961.

CONCLUSION

82.   "I will give you shepherds after my own heart" (*Jer* 3:15).

Today, this promise of God is still living and at work in the Church. At all times, she knows she is the fortunate receiver of these prophetic words. She sees them put into practice daily in so many parts of the world, or rather, in so many human hearts, young hearts in particular. On the threshold of the third millennium, and in the face of the serious and urgent needs which confront the Church and the world, she yearns to see this promise fulfilled in a new and richer way, more intensely and effectively: she hopes for an extraordinary outpouring of the Spirit of Pentecost.

The Lord's promise calls forth from the heart of the Church a prayer, that is a confident and burning petition in the love of the Father, who, just as he has sent Jesus the Good Shepherd, the Apostles, their successors and a countless host of priests, will continue to show to the men of today his faithfulness, his goodness.

And the Church is ready to respond to this grace. She feels in her heart that God's gift begs for a united and generous reply: the entire People of God should pray and work tirelessly for priestly vocations. Candidates for the priesthood should prepare themselves very conscientiously to welcome God's gift and put it into practice, knowing that the Church and the world have an absolute need of them. They should deepen their love for Christ the Good Shepherd, pattern their hearts on his, be ready to go out as his image into the highways of the world to proclaim to all mankind Christ the Way, the Truth and the Life.

I appeal especially to families. May parents, mothers in particular, be generous in giving their sons to the Lord, when he calls them to the priesthood. May they cooperate joyfully in their vocational journey, realizing that in this way they will be increasing and deepening their Christian fruitfulness in the Church and that, in a sense, they will experience the blessedness of Mary, the Virgin Mother: "Blessed are you among women, and blessed is the fruit of your womb!" (*Lk* 1: 42).

To today's young people I say: be more docile to the voice of the Spirit, let the great expectations of the Church, of mankind, resound in the depths of your hearts. Do not be afraid to open your minds to Christ the Lord who is calling. Feel his loving look upon you and respond enthusiastically to Jesus when he asks you to follow him without reserve.

The Church responds to grace through the commitment which priests make to receive that ongoing formation which is required by the dignity and responsibility conferred on them by the Sacrament of Holy Orders. All priests are called to become aware how especially urgent it is for them to receive formation at the present time: the new evangelization needs new evangelizers, and these are the priests who are serious about living their priesthood as a specific path towards holiness.

God promises the Church not just any sort of shepherds, but shepherds "after his own heart". And God's "heart" has revealed itself to us fully in the heart of Christ the Good Shepherd. Christ's heart continues today to have compassion for the multitudes and to give them the bread of truth, the bread of love, the bread of life (cf. *Mk* 6:30ff.), and it pleads to be allowed to beat in other hearts—priests' hearts: "You give them something to eat" (*Mk* 6: 37). People need to come out of their anonymity and fear. They need to be known and called by name, to walk in safety along the paths of life, to be found again if they have become lost, to be loved, to receive salvation as the supreme gift of God's love. All this is done by Jesus, the Good Shepherd—by himself and by his priests with him.

Now, as I bring this Exhortation to a close, I turn my thoughts to all aspirants to the priesthood, to seminarians and to priests who in all parts of the world—even in the most difficult and dramatic conditions, but always with the joyous struggle to be faithful to the Lord and to serve his flock unswervingly—are offering their lives daily in order that faith, hope and charity may grow in human hearts and in the history of the men and women of our day.

Dear brother priests, you do this because our Lord himself, with the strength of his Spirit, has called you to incarnate in the earthen vessels of

221

your simple lives the priceless treasure of his Good Shepherd's love.

In communion with the Synod Fathers and in the name of all the Bishops of the world and of the entire community of the Church I wish to express all the gratitude which your faithfulness and service deserve.[233]

And while I wish for all of you the grace to rekindle daily the gift of God you have received with the laying on of hands (cf. *2 Tim* 1: 6), to feel the comfort of the deep friendship which binds you to Jesus and unites you with one another, the comfort of experiencing the joy of seeing the flock of God grow in an ever greater love for him and for all people, of cultivating the tranquil conviction that the one who began in you the good work will bring it to completion at the day of Jesus Christ (cf. *Phil* 1:6); I turn with each and every one of you in *prayer to Mary, Mother and Teacher of our priesthood.*

Every aspect of priestly formation can be referred to Mary, the human being who has responded better than any other to God's call. Mary became both the servant and the disciple of the Word to the point of conceiving, in her heart and in her flesh, the Word made man, so as to give him to mankind. Mary was called to educate the one Eternal Priest, who became docile and subject to her motherly authority. With her example and intercession the Blessed Virgin keeps vigilant

---

[233] Cf. *Propositio* 40.

watch over the growth of vocations and priestly
life in the Church.

And so we priests are called to have an ever
firmer and more tender devotion to the Virgin
Mary and to show it by imitating her virtues and
praying to her often.

O Mary,
Mother of Jesus Christ and Mother of priests,
accept this title which we bestow on you
to celebrate your motherhood
and to contemplate with you the Priesthood
of your Son and of your sons,
O Holy Mother of God.

O Mother of Christ,
to the Messiah-Priest you gave a body of flesh
through the anointing of the Holy Spirit
for the salvation of the poor and the
contrite of heart;
guard priests in your heart and in the Church,
O Mother of the Saviour.

O Mother of Faith,
you accompanied to the Temple the Son of Man,
the fulfilment of the promises given to the fathers;
give to the Father for his glory
the priests of your Son,
O Ark of the Covenant.

O Mother of the Church,
in the midst of the disciples in the Upper Room
you prayed to the Spirit
for the new People and their Shepherds;

obtain for the Order of Presbyters
a full measure of gifts,
O Queen of the Apostles.

O Mother of Jesus Christ,
you were with him at the beginning
of his life and mission,
you sought the Master among the crowd,
you stood beside him when he was lifted
up from the earth
consumed as the one eternal sacrifice
and you had John, your son, near at hand;
accept from the beginning those
who have been called,
protect their growth,
in their life ministry accompany
your sons,
O Mother of Priests.
Amen.

Given in Rome, at Saint Peter's, on 25 March,
the Solemnity of the Annunciation of the Lord, in
the year 1992, the fourteenth of my Pontificate.

Joannes Paulus PP. II